Puffin Books
The Puffin Book of Brainteasers

Come to the Island of Imperfection and meet the
unreliable Shilli-Shallas and the untruthful Wotta-
Woppas; help Professor Knowall and Serjeant Simple
catch the bicycle thief; find the missing numbers and
discover the football scores – all in this collection of
150 original brainteasers, guaranteed to give you hours
of fun and entertainment!

The many different types of puzzles are arranged in
order of difficulty from the simple, one-star puzzles,
to the quite tricky three-star ones, and if you need
help to start off there are hints on how to do each
puzzle, and more detailed general suggestions if you
get stuck. Each question has a fully explained solution
and although none of the puzzles requires special
mathematical knowledge you'll soon see that you need
a little ingenuity, and must be able to think logically,
and to follow the thread of reason wherever it may
lead. One thing you can be sure of, there are no hidden
catches in the puzzles and there is no place for what is
probable or uncertain.

So why not start now and discover the compulsive
satisfaction of solving a problem little-by-little and
reaching the correct answer? Once you've done one,
you'll be sure to want to do more!

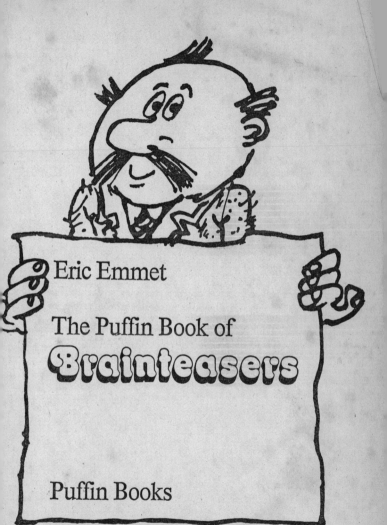

Eric Emmet

The Puffin Book of

Brainteasers

Puffin Books

Puffin Books,
Penguin Books Ltd,
Harmondsworth, Middlesex, England
Penguin Books, 625 Madison Avenue, New York,
New York 10022, U.S.A.
Penguin Books Australia Ltd,
Ringwood, Victoria, Australia
Penguin Books Canada Ltd,
2801 John Street, Markham, Ontario, Canada L3R 1B4
Penguin Books (N.Z.) Ltd,
182–190 Wairau Road, Auckland 10, New Zealand

First published 1976
Reprinted 1980, 1982

Set, printed and bound in Great Britain by
Cox & Wyman Ltd, Reading
Set in Monotype Times

To all those who helped, by encouraging, by advising, and by checking – especially my wife

Contents

Preface

Most people like solving problems. And not unnaturally most people dislike puzzles or problems which they are unable to do. I hope that this book may help many of you to experience the great pleasure and satisfaction of feeling the mind ticking over and seeing what looks at first sight to be an impossible problem, come to pieces, as it were, in your hands like knotted string or a tricky jigsaw puzzle.

But it is important not to be surprised or disappointed if at first you don't succeed. Not many of these puzzles will be solved by a blinding flash of inspiration. Most of them require a little-by-little method; you start off with something that is of itself very obvious, and indeed the only thing that is not obvious about it may be the fact that it is a possible first step towards the solution; the difficulty, as so often, is not to see that it is so, but to see that it is relevant. And in these puzzles, once you have been successful in doing a few and seeing how they work, or how the mind of the author works, it is easier to see the way to tackle the next one. At the same time you will have the great satisfaction of moving from the very simple to the really quite complicated.

The puzzles in this book are of many different kinds. There are a large number of simple addition and division sums with letters substituted for numbers, and then division sums with most of the letters missing, or with all the letters wrong. We have some cross-number puzzles, and then for those who are not so mathematically minded – although the mathematics required is very simple indeed – there are a lot of football puzzles, some using the old method of scoring, and some using a new method that has been seriously suggested but has not yet, as far as I know, been tried. There are some cricket problems too.

And then there are the odd things that happen in our factory, the adventures of Professor Knowall and Serjeant Simple, and last, but I like to think by no means least, the curious habits of the inhabitants on the Island of Imperfection.

These puzzles are arranged in order of difficulty from the very simple, one-star problems, to a few quite tricky three-star ones. In order to avoid the rather daunting feeling of seeing too many of the same kind jostling each other for places in the queue, each section (one-star to three-star) is arranged more or less at random.

For each puzzle there is a fully worked-out solution at the end of the book. And immediately after the puzzles there are a few pages of 'Hints' which will, I hope, help those of you who are unfamiliar with puzzles of this kind to get started. But the hints may not be enough, and for those who need more assistance, there are some general 'Suggestions'. I have said more about this in 'How to Use this Book'.

Many friends have helped with this book, sometimes without knowing they were doing so. I am particularly grateful to David Hall who has checked the puzzles and made many valuable suggestions, to David Wickham, headmaster of Twyford Preparatory School, and to Peter Mills, headmaster of Highfield Preparatory School, who tried some of them out on their pupils and gave me a better idea than I would otherwise have had of just how hard or easy to make them.

With a book of this kind, accurate typing matters a great deal, and I have been very fortunate in having the efficient and willing help of Mrs J. H. Preston.

And most of all I am indebted to my wife for countless suggestions for improvement and, even more important, for her support and encouragement.

How to Use this Book

Those of you who have had no experience of puzzles of this kind before may well find yourselves baffled at first. But don't be discouraged by that. However, you may well ask what you should do.

And the answer is to begin at the beginning from the 'one-star' puzzles, perhaps selecting some that particularly appeal to you, or some in which at a glance you see a starting-point, and move on from there.

This may not happen. It often doesn't. But you have other alternatives open to you.

First of all you might turn to the 'Hints' (which will be found on pages 165–70).

These consist of a few words, or sometimes a couple of lines for each puzzle, suggesting a line of attack, telling you where you might look first.

But these hints may not be enough. You might find, for example, that there are some types of puzzles – perhaps those about football – where you really do not see what is happening and you feel that the only thing to do is to start from square one. In that case I suggest that you look at pages 171–5 where football puzzles are analysed and explained more fully than is possible or desirable in the solutions.

And once you have got the idea, and have learnt to recognize in some of the puzzles some inevitably recurring themes or melodies, you will be armed with the starting-point for many puzzles and may be able to dispense with any assistance. This does not mean that the path to the solutions will then necessarily be an easy one.

You may, at first, be puzzled by the way in which the hints are arranged – first all the puzzles ending in 1, then those ending in 2, and so on. The object of this rather curious exercise is to try to make it less likely that you will be given

11

assistance when you do not want it. If the hints were arranged in the ordinary way and you wanted some assistance, say for Puzzle No. 83, it could very easily happen that you would see by accident the hint for No. 84. But you do not want that. It is possible of course that you may have already decided to do No. 93 just after 83, but as this appears several pages later it would seem unlikely! I hope the method I have used will lessen your chances of being given by accident hints which you do not want.

It may perhaps be worth saying a few words by way of a very general suggestion about the method of tackling these puzzles that is most likely to be successful.

It is fairly obvious that a random approach is not likely to produce the right answer often. The best advice I can give you is to have a method, to set out information clearly and perhaps in several different ways, and then, very often, after some trial and error, if the appropriate method has been found it will (or may!) come to pieces in your hands. But success is more likely to come if you remember how important it is to start by reading the question through very carefully indeed.

Don't expect too much too soon. This book would not be worth writing if the puzzles were too easy; and some of the harder three-star ones may really stretch your mind – I hope they do. And as a result you will get a great deal of pleasure when you solve them. Good luck!

Summary

(i) Try some puzzles without any assistance. If you are in doubt as to whether you have got them right look up your answer in the solution.

(ii) If you cannot see how and where to start look up the hint for the puzzle you are doing (pages 165–70) and see if this helps.

(iii) If you are finding the whole thing too hard try looking at the 'Suggestions' (pages 171–88). Choose a kind of puzzle in which you are particularly interested – e.g. football – and try to understand exactly how the solution is arrived at. And don't be surprised if it is necessary to read it more than once.

(iv) The fully worked-out solutions for each puzzle are on pages 189–317.

One-Star Puzzles

1 Uncle Bungle is Stung by a Couple of Bees ★

'Has it ever occurred to you,' said Uncle Bungle to me one day, 'that if I were to be stung by a couple of bees that would add up to my becoming ill.'

Not for the first time I began to think that my uncle was not quite right in the head, but I could see that he was getting rather a lot of pleasure from the fact that I couldn't understand what he was talking about.

'I,' he said, 'and a couple of bees; add them up together and I become ill.'

'Like this,' he said, and he then wrote down for me what I could see was an addition sum.

It looked like this:

$$\begin{array}{r} I \\ B\ B \\ \hline I\ L\ L \end{array}$$

When I understood what he meant I could see that it was an addition sum that even I could manage. Can you? (Each letter stands for a different digit.)

Write down the addition sum with numbers substituted for letters.

2 Football ★

Three Teams, Old Method

Three football teams – A, B and C – are to play each other once. After some, or perhaps all, of the matches had been played, a table giving some details of the number of matches played, won, lost, etc., looked like this:

	Played	Won	Lost	Drawn	Goals for	Goals against
A					3	
B		2			2	
C				1		

Find the score in each match.

3 Duggie was Dumb

On the Island of Imperfection there are three tribes – the Pukkas, who always tell the truth, the Wotta-Woppas, who never tell the truth, and the Shilli-Shallas, who make statements which are alternately true and false or false and true.

Three inhabitants of the Island, one from each tribe, were having a conversation. Their names were Bert, Charlie and Duggie. Or perhaps I shouldn't really call it a conversation because although Bert and Charlie said something, Duggie was dumb.

Bert said, 'Charlie is not a Pukka.'

Charlie said, 'Bert is not a Shilli-Shalla.'

And Duggie, as we have already remarked, said nothing.

You are told that Bert's statement was not true.

Find the tribes to which Bert, Charlie and Duggie belong.

4 Multiply by Two

In the following multiplication by two each letter stands for a different digit. *Find them.*

$$X P M$$
$$2$$
$$\overline{M A A P}$$

5 Addition

Letters for Digits, Two Numbers

Below is an addition sum with letters substituted for digits.
The same letter stands for the same digit whenever it appears,
and different letters stand for different digits.

```
    F C F
    F C B
  -------
  B B J C
```

Write out the sum with numbers substituted for letters.

6 Competition in Our Factory

I am the Managing Director of a factory in which, at the time of this story, there were only four employees.

(As the years have passed the number of workers has almost doubled and there are now seven, but this success story is another matter.)

I have always taught those who work for me the importance of competition. Work harder than the next man and run faster than him and you are more likely to be a free man. Especially if the police are after you.

In accordance with these principles my four employees, Alf, Bert, Charlie and Duggie were having a race. It was not easy to discover the result but I did manage to get a certain amount of information.

From a remark that I heard him make it appeared that Bert was not first or third, and Charlie, who does not like Alf much, could not resist boasting that he was two places above him in the race. I also discovered that Duggie was two places below Bert.

In what order did Alf, Bert, Charlie and Duggie come in their race?

22

7 Football

Three Teams, Old Method

After three football teams – A, B and C – had all played each other once, a bit of paper giving some information about the matches won, lost, drawn, and the goals for and against, was found. It read like this:

	Played	Won	Lost	Drawn	Goals for	Goals against
A	2			0	1	1
B	2	2			5	
C	2				2	

Find the score in each match.

8 Division

Letters for Digits

In the following division sum each letter stands for a different digit.

```
          d y
   d r ) r r m
         d r
         d p m
         d p m
         _____
```

Rewrite the sum with the letters replaced by digits.

9 Who Pinched My Bike ?

I think perhaps I had better introduce myself and the great detective for whom I work.

I am Serjeant Simple, and for many years now I have had the honour of working as the assistant of Professor Knowall. 'What is he a professor of?' you may ask. But perhaps it would really be better to ask what he is *not* a professor of. He has gone to the top in everything he has touched – except perhaps a few unimportant things like tying his shoe-laces and brushing his hair. And how lucky I am to work for him. Although, as a matter of fact, with all modesty, I think you will find that I am not too bad a detective myself.

But let us come to the point. My bicycle had disappeared, and after a lot of discussion, the Professor and I had come to the conclusion that taking into account the opportunities and the motives, and doing a lot of thinking about the characters of the possible suspects, it could only have been done by one of four rather suspicious characters who had recently been seen in and around our house. Their names were Clever, Idle, Loopy and Noddy and it may be taken as certain that one of them was the criminal.

We managed to see each of these four suspects alone, and they made statements as follows:

Clever said that Loopy did it.

Idle said that Loopy had told him that Noddy did it.

Loopy said that Clever did it.

Noddy said 'I know who did it but I am not saying.'

And it was at this point that the Professor's intuition and intelligence were seen at their best. Perhaps it was due to his long experience in similar cases, or to a sixth sense that other lesser mortals do not have. Whatever the explanation he said straight away that Clever and Loopy were not telling the truth but that the other two were. And I am quite sure that he was right. He always is. He also went on to say that Clever and Loopy had quite clearly not told the truth for many years now.

Who pinched my bike?

10 Addition

Letters for Digits, Two Numbers

Below is an addition sum with letters substituted for digits.
The same letter stands for the same digit wherever it appears,
and different letters stand for different digits:

```
    P Y X
    P Y X
    -----
    Y Y P
```

Write out the sum with numbers substituted for letters.

11 A Cross Number

¹	²	//////
³		⁴
⁵		

There are no 0's.

Across
1 11 goes into this
3 Each digit is greater than the one before
5 Each digit is 3 greater than the one before

Down
1 Even. Each digit is 2 less than the one before
2 Add the digits together and you get 19
4 Find me!

12 Football

Three Teams, Old Method

Three football teams – A, B and C – are to play each other
once. After some – or perhaps all of the matches have been
played a table giving some details of the number of matches
played, won, lost, etc., looked like this:

	Played	Won	Lost	Drawn	Goals for	Goals against
A				0	3	
B					5	
C			0		4	4

Find the score in each match.

13 Where was Alf?

The distance between my study and the room in which my five employees – Alf, Bert, Charlie, Duggie and Ernie – work is just about ten metres. I found it interesting therefore when I heard that they were organizing a 10-metre race. Ten metres is also curiously enough the distance between their workroom and the great outside world.

I managed to get some information about this race – Duggie, I gathered, was three places above Ernie, and Charlie was not last. Bert's and Charlie's places added up to 8, but there was no mention of Alf.

I discovered after the race the rather curious fact that the person who was last was the one who most frequently assisted me when I called for help.

There were no ties in this race.

Find the order of merit.

14 No Caps Now

There are three tribes on the Island of Imperfection – the Pukkas who always tell the truth, the Wotta-Woppas, who never tell the truth, and the Shilli-Shallas, who make statements which are alternately true and false or false and true.

In the old days, the young of each tribe wore caps, so that one knew the tribe to which the person one was talking to belonged. But things are very slack now, no caps are worn, and it is therefore very important to find people's tribes by other means – by the use of reason, for example.

It is known that A, B and C belong to different tribes, and A and C speak as follows:

A: 'I am a Wotta-Woppa.'
C: 'A is not a Shilli-Shalla.'

To what tribes do A, B and C belong?

15 Addition

Letters for Digits, Two Numbers

In the addition sum below letters have been substituted for digits. The same letter stands for the same digit wherever it appears, and different letters stand for different digits.

```
  X M A
  X X A
  -----
  M X X
```

Write out the sum with numbers substituted for letters.

16 Not as it should be

If there is one thing that my Uncle Bungle is good at it is getting things wrong.

The latest so-called addition sum which he produced for me to look at was a good example.

It looked like this:

```
    4 3
    5 7
   -----
  2 0 7
```

My uncle admitted that it was not as it should be. 'But,' he said, 'all the digits are only 1 out.'

In fact he was right in saying this. Each figure is either 1 more or 1 less than the correct figure.

Find what the addition sum ought to be.

32

17 Football

Three Teams, Old Method

Three football teams, A, B and C, were each to play each other once. After some, or perhaps all, of the matches had been played a table giving some details of matches played, won, lost, etc., looked like this:

	Played	Won	Lost	Drawn	Goals for	Goals against
A						6
B		1		0	4	0
C						3

Find the score in each match.

18 A Cross Number

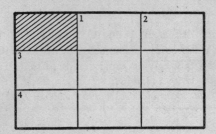

There are no 0's.

Across
1 A perfect square
3 The same when reversed; digits all even
4 Two of the digits are odd; and each one is at least 2 greater than the one before

Down
1 The sum of the digits is 15
2 Digits all even; each one is greater than the one before
3 A multiple of 7

19 Cricket

Three Teams

A, B and C have been having a cricket competition in which they have all played against each other once.

Points are awarded as follows:
to the side that wins, 10 points;
to the side that wins on the first innings in a drawn match, 6 points;
to the side that loses on the first innings in a drawn match, 2 points;
to each side in a match that is tied, 5 points;
to each side in an uncompleted match that is tied on the first innings, 4 points;
to the side that loses, 0.

A got 7 points; B got 6 points; and C got 15 points.

Find the result of each match.

Letters for Digits, Two Numbers

Below is an addition sum with letters substituted for digits.
The same letter stands for the same digit wherever it appears,
and different letters stand for different digits.

```
      P M A
      P M A
     ───────
      R P M
```

You are told that R, P and M are all even.

Write out the sum with numbers substituted for letters.

21 C is Silent

On the Island of Imperfection there are three tribes, the Pukkas, who always tell the truth, the Wotta-Woppas, who never tell the truth, and the Shilli-Shallas, who make statements which are alternately true and false or false and true.

As the reader can imagine it is always the most important part of life on the island to discover to which tribe people belong. On a recent visit I was doing some work on this with three inhabitants whom I shall call A, B and C. They have got into the habit lately of going around in threes, one from each tribe, and I am glad to say that these three were no exception.

C did not make my self-appointed job as a detective any easier by being silent, but the other two spoke as follows:

A: 'C is a Pukka.'
B: 'A is a Pukka.'

Find the tribes to which A, B and C belong.

22 Football

Three Teams, Old Method

Three football teams – A, B and C – are all to play each other
once. After some – or perhaps all – of the matches have been
played a table giving some details of the matches played, won,
lost, etc., looked like this:

	Played	Won	Lost	Drawn	Goals for	Goals against
A		2			4	
B						
C				1	1	4

Find the score in each match.

23 Ernie was Odd

Once more Alf, Bert, Charlie, Duggie and Ernie were competing against each other, really, I think, just because they couldn't stop. You are told that Bert was twice as many places above Alf as Duggie was below Charlie. And that Ernie's place was an odd number. There were no ties.

Find the order of merit.

24 Division

Some Missing Figures

Uncle Bungle, as anyone who has met him before will know, is a great one for getting things wrong. And when I saw a division sum which he had made up with some of the figures missing, I thought to myself, 'I bet he has done it again.'

But in fact, although it was not so much 'some of the figures missing' as 'nearly all of the figures missing', I discovered later that this time there were no errors. All the figures given, all three of them, were in fact correct.

The sum looked like this:

$$
\begin{array}{r}
-\,1 \\
4-\,)\overline{-\,-\,-\,9} \\
-\,- \\
-\,- \\
-\,- \\
-
\end{array}
$$

Find the complete sum.

25 Addition

Letters for Digits, Two Numbers

Below is an addition sum with letters substituted for digits.
The same letter stands for the same digit wherever it appears,
and different letters stand for different digits.

```
  Q X X Y
  A P X X
---------
P M Y P Q
```

Write out the sum with numbers substituted for letters.

26 Football

Four Teams, Old Method

Four football teams – A, B, C and D – are to play each other once. After some of the matches have been played a table giving some details of matches played, won, lost, etc., looked like this:

	Played	Won	Lost	Drawn	Goals for	Goals against
A						3
B	1					
C	1				4	3
D						2

Find the score in each match.

27 A Cross Number

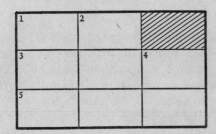

There are no 0's.

Across
1 The square of an even number
3 The same when reversed
5 A multiple of 1 Down

Down
1 Each digit is 2 greater than the one before
2 See 4 Down
4 The sum of the digits is the same as the sum of the digits of 2 Down

28 One of Each, and They All Speak ★

On the Island of Imperfection there are three tribes – the Pukkas, who always tell the truth, the Wotta-Woppas, who never tell the truth, and the Shilli-Shallas, who make statements which are alternately true and false or false and true.

Once more it is nice to be able to record that A, B and C, with whom this story deals, all belong to different tribes. Sometimes in the past it has been difficult to get them all to contribute, that is, to say something about themselves or the others, but this time they were very friendly indeed and they all talked.

As follows:

A: 'I am a Shilli-Shalla.'
B: 'A is a Pukka.'
C: 'B belongs to a less truthful tribe than A.'

Find the tribes to which A, B and C belong.

29 Cricket

Three Teams

A, B and C have all played each other once at cricket.
  Points are awarded as follows:
to the side that wins, 10;
to the side that wins on the first innings in a drawn match, 6;
to the side that loses on the first innings in a drawn match, 2;
to each side for a tie, 5;
to each side for a tie on the first innings in a drawn match, 4;
to the side that loses, 0.
  A, B and C got 12, 10 and 4 points respectively.

Find the result of each match.

30 Addition

Letters for Digits, Two Numbers

Below is an addition sum with letters substituted for digits.
The same letter stands for the same digit wherever it appears,
and different letters stand for different digits.

$$
\begin{array}{ccc}
M & B & M \\
B & B & M \\
\hline
E & X & X \\
\end{array}
$$

Write out the sum with numbers substituted for letters.

31 Football

Three Teams, Old Method

Three football teams – A, B and C – are each to play each other once. After some, or perhaps all, of the matches have been played a table giving some details of the number of matches played, won, lost, etc., looked like this:

	Played	Won	Lost	Drawn	Goals for	Goals against
A		1			4	
B					6	
C				1	4	4

Find the score in each match.

32 Division

Letters for Digits

In the following division sum each letter stands for a different digit.

```
            z e p
      p d ) y x q x z
            d b
          ─────
          p y x
          z h s
          ─────
            y b z
            y y y
            ─────
              p y
            ─────
```

Write out the sum with the letters replaced by digits.

33 A Cross Number

¹	²	³
⁴		
▨	⁵	

There are no 0's.

Across
1 Digits all odd, and each one greater than the one before
4 Digits all even, and each one less than the one before
5 The sum of the digits is a multiple of 5

Down
1 A perfect square
2 Each digit is greater than the one before
3 The sum of the digits is 19

34 Addition

Letters for Digits, Three Numbers

Below is an addition sum with letters substituted for digits.
The same letter stands for the same digit wherever it appears,
and different letters stand for different digits.

```
    Y  M  B
    Y  M  B
    Y  M  B
  _____
  B  B  B  Y
```

Write out the sum with numbers substituted for letters.

35 A was Absent

There are three tribes on the Island of Imperfection – the Pukkas, who always tell the truth, the Wotta-Woppas, who never tell the truth, and the Shilli-Shallas, who make statements which are alternately true and false or false and true.

I have not been on the island for long, and therefore have not had much experience of their customs, but it was particularly important for me to discover the tribes to which three people, A, B and C belonged. All I knew was that there was one representative from each tribe, and clearly what I had to do was to try to get them talking. The position however was not made easier by the fact that for some reason A was not around, and so I could only get statements from B and C.

They spoke as follows:

B: 'A is more truthful than C.'
C: 'B is a Pukka.'

Find the tribes to which A, B and C belong.

36 Football

Three Teams, Old Method

Three football teams, A, B and C had each played each other once. Below is a table giving some details of these matches.

	Played	Won	Lost	Drawn	Goals for	Goals against
A	2			1		
B	2	1			4	4
C	2				3	0

Find the score in each match.

37 Division

Some Missing Figures

A division sum.

```
          – 3
– –)– – 8 –
    – – –
    ─────
     8 –
     – –
     ───
```

Find the missing digits.

38 Stealing, Breaking and Stopping ★

No lives were lost in the crimes with which this story deals, but it is interesting because it is such a good example of the speed with which Professor Knowall's mind works.

The Managing Director of a small factory, who is an old friend of the Professor, had asked him for his assistance.

It seemed that four of his employees, Alf, Bert, Charlie and Duggie were suspected of three rather curious crimes. What had been happening, not once but many times, was that windows had been broken, clocks had been stopped and pencils had been stolen. These misdemeanours were so curious that I thought it would be wise to consult someone who was an expert on the way in which people's minds work. But I had, of course, forgotten that this branch of knowledge was one of the many things which the Professor is a professor of!

'I think you can rely on me, Serjeant Simple,' he said rather crisply, 'to combine detection with psychology in sorting this matter out. I remember that there was a similar case on the Island of Never-Never, and from my experience there and elsewhere I would say that one thing is quite certain, namely, that this is a one-man, one-crime job. Whenever a window

has been broken one person, and one person only, has been responsible for it and it is part of the mental illness from which these unfortunate men suffer that if they are in a situation where, for example, there is a clock to be stopped then it will be stopped; and the same thing is true of the other crimes.'

Fortunately the Managing Director of the factory was able to give us a certain amount of precise information.

Apparently in a situation in which Alf, Charlie and Duggie were present, and it was possible to do any of the crimes, a window was broken and a clock was stopped.

In a similar situation in which Alf, Bert and Charlie were present, a pencil was stolen and a window was broken. And in a situation in which only Alf and Duggie were present, a clock was stopped.

It is obviously difficult for readers who were not present to get the atmosphere of a superbrain ticking over at high speed, which I was able to get, and to enjoy. Let me just say that the Professor solved the problem in less time than it would have taken to break a window.

Assuming that one man specializes in breaking windows, one in stopping clocks and one in stealing pencils, find which of the four men was responsible for each of the three crimes.

39 Only One Out

'Well, they are only 1 out,' said Uncle Bungle.

As though that mattered. For he does not seem to realize that if they are wrong they are wrong.

He was referring to a subtraction sum in which, whether by accident or design, all the figures were wrong. They were all 1 more or 1 less than they should have been. Some people say that my Uncle is careless and that he does not see very well, but my own view is that he likes teasing people by getting things wrong.

The figures in Uncle Bungle's subtraction sum were as follows:

$$
\begin{array}{r}
2\,1\,6\,6\,4\,8 \\
9\,0\,1\,3\,5 \\
\hline
1\,3\,7\,8\,0 \\
\hline
\end{array}
$$

Find the correct figures.

40 Addition

Letters for Digits, Three Numbers

Below is an addition sum with letters substituted for digits.
The same letter stands for the same digit wherever it appears,
and different letters stand for different digits. There are no 1's.

```
    R A X
    A A X
    X A X
  -------
    M P M
```

Write out the sum with numbers substituted for letters.

41 Football

Three Teams, New Method

In the new football league, points are given for goals scored as well as for wins and draws. 10 points are given for a win, 5 points for a draw and 1 point for each goal scored, whatever the result of the match.

Three teams – A, B and C – have each played each other once. And the success of this new method can be seen from the fact that in each game both sides scored at least 1 goal – and more and better goals is the main object of the exercise.

The total number of points for each team was:

A – 9
B – 26
C – 7

Find the score in each match.

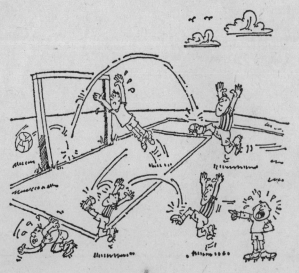

42 A Cross Number

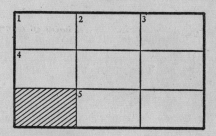

There are no 0's.

Across
1 An even number when reversed
4 Each digit is greater than the one before
5 3 times 1 Down

Down
1 See 5 Across
2 The same when reversed
3 5 times 5 Across

43 Not Talking Much

The three inhabitants of the Island of Imperfection with whom this story deals are not in the habit of talking much, and on this occasion they only made one remark each.

There are, of course, three tribes on the Island – the Pukkas, who always tell the truth, the Wotta-Woppas, who never tell the truth, and the Shilli-Shallas, who make statements which are alternately true and false or false and true. Each tribe has one representative among the three, whom we shall call A, B and C.

They speak as follows:

A: 'B is a Shilli-Shalla.'
B: 'C is not a Wotta-Woppa.'
C: 'A is a Pukka.'

What are their tribes?

44 Division

Letters for Digits

In the following division sum each letter stands for a different digit.

```
              x c d y
    n m ) n n r m b a
          n b r
          n b m
          d n
          n y b
          n n c
              m a
              y p
              d
```

Write out the sum with the letters replaced by digits.

45 Addition

Letters for Digits, Two Numbers

Below is an addition sum with letters substituted for digits.
The same letter stands for the same digit wherever it appears,
and different letters stand for different digits.

$$
\begin{array}{ccc}
Q & Q & Z \\
L & Q & Z \\
\hline
E & L & L \\
\end{array}
$$

Write out the sum with numbers substituted for letters.

46 Football

Four Teams, Old Method

A, B, C and D are each to play each other once at football. After some of the matches had been played a table giving some of the figures of matches played, won, lost, drawn, etc., looked like this:

	Played	Won	Lost	Drawn	Goals for	Goals against	Points
A	1					1	
B	1				3		2
C					2	2	
D	3				4		3

(2 points are given for a win, and 1 point for a draw.)

Find the score in each match.

47 Who Does What in Our Factory ★

This story is about the early days of our factory, just after we had made the great expansion to seven employees.

Alf, Bert, Charlie, Duggie, Ernie, Fred and George are their names; and their jobs, not necessarily respectively, are the Door-Opener, the Door-Shutter, the Door-Knob-Polisher, the Bottle-Washer, the Welfare Officer, the Sweeper-Upper and last but, in spite of what some people say, not least, the Worker.

Alf was not the Bottle-Washer or the Worker; and Fred was not the Door-Knob-Polisher, the Door-Opener or the Worker.

Bert was either the Welfare Officer, the Door-Shutter or the Sweeper-Upper; and Duggie was either the Door-Knob-Polisher or the Sweeper-Upper.

The Door-Shutter was not Bert, Charlie or George; and the Sweeper-Upper was not Bert, Ernie or Fred. But the Door-Opener was either Alf, Charlie or Fred.

The Door-Knob-Polisher was not Charlie, Duggie or George; and the Worker was not Charlie or George.

Find each of my employees' occupations.

48 Pocket-Money on the Island of Imperfection ★

We are back again on the Island of Imperfection where there are three tribes – the Pukkas, who always tell the truth, the Wotta-Woppas, who never tell the truth, and the Shilli-Shallas, who make statements which are alternately true and false or false and true.

They are happy people on the island, and on the whole they look forward to the future with pleasure. Perhaps that is why they call their money Hopes.

In a recent inquiry to find out something about pocket-money on the island, three boys – one from each tribe, whom we shall call A, B and C – made two statements, each in accordance with their tribal rules. As follows:

A: (1) 'My pocket-money is more than B's.'
   (2) 'B's pocket-money is 50 Hopes.'
B: (1) 'A is a Shilli-Shalla.'
   (2) 'A's pocket-money is twice C's.'
C: (1) 'B's pocket-money is more than A's.'
   (2) 'A's second statement is false.'

I was informed by a very reliable authority that B's first statement was true.

How much pocket-money do A, B and C receive, and to what tribes do they belong?

49 Uncle Bungle Shows that He Can Get Division Sums Wrong Too!

Uncle Bungle always wants to do better than other people or sometimes just better than himself. We have seen a subtraction sum of his with all the figures wrong and he has now produced a long division sum with all the figures wrong too. Does he do it on purpose, I wonder, or can he just not help it?

Perhaps we shall never know the answer to this question but it is at least rather odd that in this sum, like the addition sum, all the digits are just 1 out, that is to say they are 1 more or 1 less than they should be.

The sum looks like this:

$$
\begin{array}{r}
29 \\
84\overline{)2223} \\
62 \\
\hline
693 \\
493 \\
\hline
\end{array}
$$

Find the correct figures.

Letters for Digits, Two Numbers

Below is an addition sum with letters substituted for digits.
The same letter stands for the same digit wherever it appears,
and different letters stand for different digits.

```
    R P A P
    A B B M
  ─────────
  R R R R P
```

Write out the sum with numbers substituted for letters.

51 A Cross Number

There are no 0's.

Across
1 An even number, and a multiple of 9
3 Digits all even
4 Digits all different, and the sum of the digits is 11

Down
1 Even. Sum of the digits is greater than 15
2 Each digit is greater than the one before
3 A perfect cube

52 Football

Three Teams, New Method

In order to encourage more goals in football a new method has been devised in which not only the result counts but also the number of goals scored.

In this method 10 points are awarded for a win, 5 points for a draw, and 1 point for each goal scored whatever the result of the match.

In a recent competition between three teams – A, B and C – in which they all played each other once, the points which each team got were as follows:

A – 22
B – 15
C – 8

In each match each side scored at least 1 goal, but not more than 7 were scored by both teams. B did not lose a match.

Find the score in each game.

53 The Good Worker

At the time with which this story deals three of the employees in our factory – Ernie, Fred and George – had the jobs, not necessarily respectively, of Door-Opener, Door-Shutter and Worker.

Perhaps because of the in-and-out nature of their jobs the Door-Opener and the Door-Shutter had got, I'm afraid, into the habit of telling lies. But not the Worker. He did a good job and he told the truth.

They spoke as follows:

Ernie: 'George is the Door-Shutter.'

Fred: 'Ernie is the Door-Opener.'

George: 'Fred is the Worker.'

Find the jobs of my three employees.

54 Still Only One Out

In his latest rather curious-looking subtraction sum Uncle Bungle makes no secret of what he is trying to do. The object of the exercise as far as he is concerned is to deceive and to conceal.

But all the figures are only 1 out, and I am sure that my readers will be intelligent enough to call Uncle Bungle's bluff, as it were, and to produce the correct figures.

The incorrect figures were:

$$
\begin{array}{r}
2\ 9\ 1\ 0 \\
1\ 4\ 9\ 7 \\
\hline
2\ 1\ 0\ 6
\end{array}
$$

Find the correct figures.

55 Addition

Letters for Digits, Two Numbers

Below is an addition sum with letters substituted for digits.
The same letter stands for the same digit whenever it appears,
and different letters stand for different digits.

```
      D T S U
      D N N U
    ─────────
    U T D N T
```

Write out the sum with numbers substituted for letters.

56 Division

Some Missing Figures

A division sum.

```
              3 - -
    - - ) - - 0 - 0
          - -
          ─────
          - -
          - -
          ─────
          - - -
          - - -
          ─────
```

Find the missing digits.

57 Football

Three Teams, Old Method

Three football teams – A, B and C – are each to play each other once. After some, or perhaps all, of the matches had been played a piece of paper giving some details of matches played, won, lost, drawn, etc., looked like this:

	Played	Won	Lost	Drawn	Goals for	Goals against	Points
A		0					
B					5	3	4
C						2	0

(2 points are awarded for a win and 1 point for a draw.)

Find the score in each match.

58 The Breathless B

We have got accustomed over the years to B being in rather a hurry, but I have never known him more breathless than he was the other day. It might be said, I suppose, that this is all part of the imperfection of the island on which we live.

There are three tribes on this island, the Pukkas, who always tell the truth, the Wotta-Woppas, who never tell the truth, and the Shilli-Shallas, who make statements which are alternately true and false or false and true.

Three members of the island, one from each tribe, have been having a conversation which was in fact rather spoilt by the breathlessness of B to which I have been referring. In fact he did not utter.

The other two make statements as follows:
A: 'I am a Wotta-Woppa.'
C: 'A is a Shilli-Shalla.'

Find the tribes to which A, B and C belong.

59 Letters for Digits

A Multiplication

Below is a multiplication sum with letters substituted for numbers. The same letter stands for the same digit wherever it appears, and different letters stand for different digits.

```
    Z Y Y P M
            M
  _____
  A A Z E Y M
```

You are told that Y is half of M, and that P is less than Y.

Find the digits for which the letters stand.

60 Addition

Letters for Digits, Two Numbers

Below is an addition sum with letters substituted for digits. The same letter stands for the same digit wherever it appears, and different letters stand for different digits.

```
    M B B
  S K K B
  _____
  M W W X K
```

Write out the sum with numbers substituted for letters.

61 Division

Letters for Digits

In the following division sum each letter stands for a different digit.

```
              r x g d
      x g) t h s f g g
            t r r
            ─────
            t x f
            t f j
            ─────
              d d g
              d t g
              ─────
                t f g
                s d
                ───
                x r
```

Write out the sum with the letters replaced by digits.

62 Football

Four Teams, New Method

The new method of rewarding goals in football matches, irrespective of who wins, is becoming more and more popular.

Under this method 10 points are awarded for a win, 5 points for a draw, and 1 point for each goal that the team scores, irrespective of the result of the match. It is interesting to notice the extent to which more goals continue to be scored; in the latest competition, each side scored at least one goal in every match.

The four teams, A, B, C and D are eventually all going to play each other once. The situation when all but two matches had been played was as follows:

A – 20 points
B – 4 points
C – 1 point
D – 30 points.

Find the score in each match.

76

63 Who was X?

★

When one of my employees told me the other day that he had come fourth in a fifty metre race I must say that I was rather surprised. X, as I shall call him for the moment, had always been the slowest in every way of the seven members of our factory, and I could not imagine him coming anywhere but last in any competition.

But it was not long before I discovered that last in fact was where he had come, for there were only four people in the race – namely Alf, Charlie, Ernie and George.

But the reader might like to have enough information to find out exactly what did happen.

Charlie was as many places behind Ernie as George was before Alf.

Ernie was not first and Alf was not second.

Who was X? And in what order did they all come in the race?

64 A Cross Number

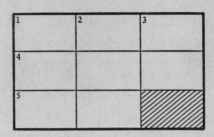

There are no 0's.

Across
1 5 Across multiplied by 7
4 Each digit is greater than the one before
5 A multiple of 19

Down
1 Sum of digits is 8
2 An even number
3 A multiple of 13

Three Teams

A, B and C have all played each other once at cricket. Points are awarded as follows:
to the side that wins, 10;
to the side that wins on the first innings in a drawn match, 6;
to the side that loses on the first innings in a drawn match, 2;
to each side for a tie, 5;
to the side that loses, 0.

A, B and C got 11, 10 and 7 points respectively.

Find the result of each match.

66 Division ★

Some Missing Figures

A division sum.

```
        - 5 -
    - -)6 - - -
       - -
       - - -
         - -
        - 7 -
        - - -
```

Find the missing digits.

67 Addition

Letters for Digits, Two Numbers

Below is an addition sum with letters substituted for digits.
The same letter stands for the same digit wherever it appears,
and different letters stand for different digits.

```
  Z B B
  B Y B
  -----
  C Z Z
```

Write out the sum with numbers substituted for letters.

68 Football

Four Teams, Consecutive Saturdays

Four football teams – A, B, C and D – all play each other once
on three consecutive Saturdays.

The goals scored by each of them are as follows:

	A	B	C	D
Sat. 1	1	3	2	2
Sat. 2	4	3	0	1
Sat. 3	4	0	4	1

The total number of goals scored *against* them were as
follows:
against A – 5
against B – 8
against C – 2
against D – 7.

Find the score in each match.

69 The Running-Backward Race ★

The workers in my factory realize very well that in order to fit themselves for a modern industrial world they must compete. It seems sensible to them that they should get practice in this by competing against each other.

The latest competition I have organized has been a running-backward race, in which Alf, Bert, Charlie, Duggie and Ernie have been trying to see who can move fastest in the wrong direction.

Duggie beat Bert by as many places as Alf beat Charlie, and Bert beat Charlie.

Ernie was not first or third, and Bert was not second.

Find the order in which they came in the race.

70 More Pocket-Money on the ★ Island of Imperfection

There are three tribes on the Island of Imperfection – the Pukkas, who always tell the truth, the Wotta-Woppas, who never tell the truth, and the Shilli-Shallas, who make statements which are alternately true and false or false and true.

Three boys on the island – one from each tribe, whom we shall call A, B and C, each make two statements. My spies, whom I trust absolutely, told me that B's first statement was false. (The units of money are Hopes.)

They speak as follows:

A: (1) 'B's pocket-money is twice C's.'
   (2) 'The least of our three pocket-monies is 30 Hopes.'
B: (1) 'A is a Shilli-Shalla.'
   (2) 'My pocket-money is three times C's.'
C: (1) 'I am a Wotta-Woppa.'
   (2) 'My pocket-money is three-quarters of A's.'

Find out how much pocket-money A, B and C receive, and the tribes to which they belong.

Two-Star Puzzles

71 Football

Four Teams, Old Method

Four football teams – A, B, C and D – are all to play each other once.

After some – or perhaps all – of the matches have been played a table giving some details of the matches played, won, lost, etc., looked like this:

	Played	Won	Lost	Drawn	Goals for	Goals against
A		0		1	3	3
B						
C	3				7	5
D			0	0	2	1

Find the score in each match.

Letters for Digits, Two Numbers

Below is an addition sum with letters substituted for digits.
The same letter stands for the same digit wherever it appears,
and different letters stand for different digits.

$$\begin{array}{ccccc}
 & R & A & A & P \\
 & G & G & A & P \\
\hline
P & M & B & M & R \\
\end{array}$$

Write out the sum with numbers substituted for letters.

73 All is Confusion – but the Bottle-Washer was Third

I fear that as Managing Director of our factory I seem to have lost my touch. Events have happened so quickly and my workers – Alf, Bert, Charlie, Duggie and Ernie – seem to have changed their jobs so frequently that I really hardly know who is what. I do know, however, that their jobs at the moment are – in no particular order – those of Bottle-Washer, Door-Opener, Door-Shutter, Door-Knob-Polisher and last, and unfortunately rather often least, Worker.

They have been having a competition amongst each other for something or other (and it may give you some idea of the state I am in that I really don't know what) and I have been able to get hold of a certain amount of information about this. I do know that in accordance with the long-standing custom of the company there were no ties.

The information that I was able to get hold of was as follows:

1 Bert was three places above the Door-Opener, who was below Alf.
2 None of the three doormen was fifth.
3 The Door-Knob-Polisher was three places above Charlie.
4 Duggie was one place below the Door-Shutter.
5 Ernie's place was even.
6 The Bottle-Washer was third.

I hope that from this information you will be able to discover in what order Alf, Bert, Charlie, Duggie and Ernie came in this competition and what their jobs were.

In the following multiplication each letter stands for a different digit. *Find them.*

$$
\begin{array}{r}
\text{C B D F} \\
\times \quad 4 \\
\hline
\text{D F D E D}
\end{array}
$$

75 Cause and Effect

It is perhaps rather difficult to know what Professor Knowall is best at. But one thing at which he is certainly very good indeed (and indeed as a detective he should be) is the tracing of cause and effect.

'Remember, my dear Serjeant Simple,' as he has so often said to me, 'that generally speaking the same cause has usually the same effect or effects. If I stand in the rain without any clothes I shall get wet. But I may also get wet in a lot of other ways, for example by diving into the sea. In other words, the same event may be preceded by many different causes.'

It was a great piece of luck that next day I had a chance to show my new cause-and-effect skill in a rather tricky piece of detection. I won't burden the reader with the details, but will put the facts down just as the Professor suggested I should with the causes followed by the possible effects.

To cut all sorts of long stories short there were six possible causes (A, B, C, D, E, F) and they were followed by four possible effects; fortunately there was every reason to believe that each effect had just one single cause.

The details were as follows:

A, C, F were followed by q and r.

B, C, D, F were followed by s and r.

B, D, E were followed by p and s.

A, D, E, F were followed by p and q.

What were the causes of p, q, r, s.

Uncle Bungle sings a song:
'One of these is surely wrong.
Choose, as you'll appreciate:
Two or Four or Six or Eight?'

```
                2 -
    4 -)- - - 8
        - - -
        -----
          - -
          6 -
          ---
```

Which of these figures was 'surely wrong'?

Find the correct division sum.

77 Football

Three Teams, Old Method

Three football teams – A, B and C – are to play each other once. After some – or perhaps all – of the matches have been played a piece of paper giving some details of matches played, won, lost, etc., looked like this:

	Played	Won	Lost	Drawn	Goals for	Goals against
A					5	4
B				1	2	
C					6	4

Find the score in each match.

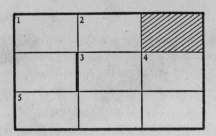

There are no 0's.

Across
1 A factor of 3 Across
3 A perfect square
5 The sum of the digits is 12. They are all even and all different

Down
1 A multiple of 4 Down
2 Each digit is greater than the one before
4 A perfect square

79 Addition

Letters for Digits, Two Numbers

Below is an addition sum with letters substituted for digits.
The same letter stands for the same digit wherever it appears,
and different letters stand for different digits:

```
    E H R G
    M H R G
  ─────────
  M D M E E
```

Write out the sum with numbers substituted for letters.

80 A Competition

Alf, Bert, Charlie, Duggie and Ernie have been having a competition with each other, in which there are no ties.

You are told that Alf was as many places above Bert as Duggie was above Ernie; and that neither Charlie nor Ernie were third or fifth.

Find their order.

81 Division

Figures All Wrong

In the following, obviously incorrect, division sum the
pattern is correct, but all the figures are 1 out, that is they are
1 more or 1 less than the correct figures. The sum comes out
exactly.

```
          3 8
   2 3 ) 8 7 5
         7 7
         ─────
         2 1 5
         4 1 5
         ─────
```

Find the correct figures.

82 Football

Three Teams, New Method

What attracts people to watch football is goals being scored. And the authorities have been thinking for a long time of methods whereby the scoring of more goals might be encouraged.

One suggestion that has been made involves a change in the way that points are awarded. The idea is that 10 points should be awarded for a win, 5 points for a draw, and 1 point for each goal scored, whatever the result of the match. Therefore even if you are losing 0–5 and have no hope of winning, a goal scored might make all the difference between promotion and non-promotion.

This method was tried out on a small scale and its success can be judged from the fact that each side scored at least one goal in every match. There were only three sides playing and eventually they are all going to play each other once. A had scored 8 points, B had scored 14 points, and C had scored 9 points.

Find the score in each match.

98

83 Serjeant Simple Loses his Wallet

I could not think where I had left it. My wallet, I mean. It contained several things of sentimental value and also a little bit of money in which I am quite interested.

Professor Knowall was not being very helpful.

'If you can't find your own wallet, how are you going to find criminals, my dear Serjeant Simple?' he said.

And although I was pretty certain that he knew where it was, all I could persuade him to do was to give me a few clues. They went like this:

(1) If you don't fail to find your wallet it's because you haven't looked in the deep freeze.

(2) If you can't find your wallet it's because you haven't looked behind the desk.

(3) You can't both find your wallet and not fail to look in the cycle shed.

I am afraid this was too much for me, but perhaps the reader may be able to make suggestions as to where I should look for my wallet.

84 Addition

Letters for Digits, Two Numbers

Below is an addition sum with letters substituted for digits.
The same letter stands for the same digit wherever it appears,
and different letters stand for different digits.

$$
\begin{array}{cccccc}
Z & Z & Y & B & R & R \\
Z & Z & Y & Z & R & R \\
\hline
Y & Y & X & X & Q & Z \\
\hline
\end{array}
$$

Write out the sum with numbers substituted for letters.

85 A Cross Number

¹	²	▨
³		⁴
⁵		

There are no 0's.

Across

1 A factor of 3 Across
3 An odd number. Each digit is greater than the one before
5 1 Down multiplied by an even number.

Down

1 See 5 Across
2 We seem to have this somewhere else
4 A perfect square

Some Missing Figures

A division sum.

```
              3 - - -
    - - ) - - - - 5 -
          - -
          ‾‾‾‾
          - - -
            - -
            ‾‾‾
            - -
            - -
            ‾‾
```

Find the missing digits.

87 They All Compete

It is not often that I make all the seven members of our factory staff compete against each other, but when it came to deciding which of them was to have the honour of representing us in the Common Market there really was no alternative. It is not necessary to tell you about the examination I gave them, except to say that I was testing things about their intelligence and character which they did not even know they had. But you might be interested to hear some details of the results.

Bert was as many places above Duggie as Alf was below Fred. Duggie's and Charlie's places were even and Alf's was odd. Ernie was below Alf and Fred was below Duggie. But I am afraid I can give no information about George's place.

Can you find the order in which they came in the examination?

88 Football

Four Teams, Old Method

Four football teams – A, B, C and D – were each to play each other once. After they had each played two matches some details of the matches played, won, lost, etc., looked like this:

	Played	Won	Lost	Drawn	Goals for	Goals against
A	2			1		4
B	2			1	3	0
C	2				2	7
D	2			0		2

Find the score in each match.

Letters for Digits, Two Numbers

In the addition sum below letters have been substituted for digits. The same letter stands for the same digit wherever it appears, and different letters stand for different digits.

```
  B Y B
  M Y B
  -----
  Y M M
```

Write out the sum with numbers substituted for letters.

90 The Factory Dinner-Party ★★

This story is about the occasion, many years ago now, when the five original workers in my factory were, for the first time, to be paid for the work which they did. Before this they had had hopes and promises, free suppers, and a permanent invitation to sleep in the stables, but no cash. After all it seemed reasonable to wait until we had actually sold some of our products. But now this great event had actually happened, and if anything ever called for a celebration, this was surely it.

So my five employees – Alf, Bert, Charlie, Duggie and Ernie, whose jobs at that time, but in no particular order, were the Bottle-Washer, the Door-Opener, the Door-Shutter, the Welfare Officer and the Worker – were sitting round a circular table waiting for their employer, that is myself, to give them dinner.

You might be interested to know just how they were sitting and what their jobs were.

No two men, the initial letters of whose names were next to each other in the alphabet, were sitting next to each other at the table, and Charlie does not have Alf sitting on his right.

Bert is sitting between the Welfare Officer and the Door-Shutter, and the two doormen (the Door-Shutter and the Door-Opener), one of whom is Duggie, are not sitting next to each other. You are also told that Alf is not the Bottle-Washer.

Show in a diagram where my employees were sitting and what their jobs were.

91 Division

Letters for Digits

In the following division sum each letter stands for a different digit.

```
          d k g b
   d h )g d n s f s
        g g n
        s f s
        g h k
          n f
          d h
          d g s
          d g s
```

Find the sum with the letters replaced by digits.

¹	²	³
⁴		
////	⁵	

There are no 0's.

Across
1 Each digit is greater than the one before
4 The same when reversed. Odd
5 A perfect square

Down
1 A perfect square
2 Sum of digits is 16
3 Each digit is greater than the one before

A Multiplication

In the following multiplication sum letters have been substituted for digits, and of course the same letters stand for the same digits whenever they occur, and different letters stand for different digits.

$$
\begin{array}{r}
\text{P M M T P} \\
\text{P} \\
\hline
\text{N P T R P T}
\end{array}
$$

You are told that P = 2T.

Find the digits for which the letters stand.

94 Uncle Bungle's Football Puzzle

My Uncle Bungle is very keen on games, especially on football, and now that he is a pretty elderly gentleman he has taken to making up puzzles about his favourite game.

In his latest one about four teams, A, B, C and D, who are eventually going to play each other once, I'm afraid that a large number of the figures have just been left out. I never quite know whether this is due to my uncle's carelessness (and he is indeed a very careless man), or whether he is being rather clever in giving just the amount of information that is needed.

Whatever it is you might like to find out the score in the matches that have been played between four teams A, B, C and D.

The information that my uncle gave was as follows:

	Played	Won	Lost	Drawn	Goals for	Goals against
A		2			2	
B			0	0	4	3
C					5	3
D	3					

Find the score in each match.

Letters for Digits, Two Numbers

Below is an addition sum with letters substituted for digits.
The same letter stands for the same digit wherever it appears,
and different letters stand for different digits.

```
  R X E K P P
  R X X R P P
  ───────────
  H R B H P H
```

Write out the sum with numbers substituted for letters.

96 The Lower the Truer ★★

Although we may not have said much about it in the past, great importance has always been attached to our 'personal numbers' on the Island of Imperfection. There can be a large number of John Smiths even on our small island, but there will be only one 3968.

There are three tribes on the island, the Pukkas, who always tell the truth, the Wotta-Woppas, who never tell the truth, and the Shilli-Shallas, whose statements are alternately true and false or false and true.

The three members of the island with whom this story deals, one from each tribe, have personal numbers which are not in fact very large. It so happens on this occasion that the more truthful a man's tribe is, the lower is his personal number. But there is no general rule about this.

We shall call them A, B and C. They speak as follows:

A: (1) 'C's number is even.'
　　(2) 'B is a Pukka.'
B: (1) 'My number is 20.'
　　(2) 'C is a Shilli-Shalla.'
C: (1) 'A's number is 5 more or 5 less than mine.'
　　(2) 'A's number is not a multiple of 6.'

You are told that B's first remark is true.

Find the tribe to which each man belongs, and his personal number.

113

97 Cricket

Three Teams

A, B and C have all played each other once at cricket.
   Points are awarded as follows:
to the side that wins, 10;
to the side that wins on the first innings in a drawn match, 6;
to the side that loses on the first innings in a drawn match, 2;
to each side for a tie, 5;
to each side for a tie on the first innings in a drawn match, 4;
to the side that loses, 0.
   I was told that A got 3 points, that B got 11, and that C got
13. But I learnt subsequently that two of these figures were
wrong, though neither of them were more than 2 out. I was
also able to discover that no match was won.

   Find the result of each match.

Figures All Wrong

In the following, obviously incorrect, division sum, the pattern is correct, but all the figures are 1 out, that is they are 1 more or 1 less than the correct figures. The sum comes out exactly.

```
        3 4
  1 4)6 1 8
      5 5
      ───
      7 8
      5 8
      ───
      ───
```

Find the correct figures.

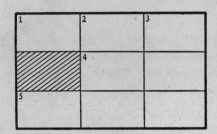

There are no 0's.

Across

1 An even number. It contains the largest even digit in the puzzle

4 The square of an odd number

5 The sum of the digits is 13

Down

2 5 times 4 Across

3 An even number. Each digit is greater than the one before by the same amount

100 Football

Four Teams, Old Method

Four football teams – A, B, C and D – are all to play each other once. After some of the matches have been played a table giving some details of the number of matches played, won, lost, etc., looked like this:

	Played	Won	Lost	Drawn	Goals for	Goals against
A				2		
B			1		4	
C				0	1	1
D	1					3

Find the score in each match.

101 The Ladies have a Competition

The men on the Island of Imperfection are always having fun-and-games and competitions, but this time it is the turn of the ladies.

There are three tribes on the island, the Pukkas, who always tell the truth, the Wotta-Woppas, who never tell the truth, and the Shilli-Shallas, who make statements which are alternately true and false or false and true.

This story deals with six ladies who are competing against each other for some very important prize which will, I am told, include a choice of husbands. But exactly what the tests are which produce the final order of merit (in which there are no ties) I'm afraid I am not able to tell you.

The names of the ladies are Agnes and Angela who belong to the same tribe, Belinda and Beryl who belong to another tribe, and Clarissa and Clementine who belong to the third tribe.

Agnes, Belinda and Clarissa speak as follows:

A: (1) 'The girls who were first and last were both Pukkas.'
   (2) 'Beryl was two places higher than Belinda.'
B: (1) 'Clementine was last.'
   (2) 'Clarissa is a Pukka.'
C: (1) 'Clementine was third.'
   (2) 'Agnes is a Shilli-Shalla.'

Find the tribes to which they all belong and as much as you can about their order of merit.

102 Addition

Letters for Digits, Three Numbers

In the addition sum below the digits have been replaced by letters. The same letter stands for the same digit wherever it appears, and different letters stand for different digits.

```
  D A R M M M
  P H M P M M
  R M G M M M
-------------
F J K A D D
```

Write out the sum with numbers substituted for letters.

103 Division

Letters for Digits

In the following division sum each letter stands for a different digit.

```
        b h
    ---------
h f ) m b d
      m h
      -----
        x d
        h f
        -----
          f
```

Rewrite the sum with the letters replaced by digits.

104 Multiply by 3

In the following multiplication each letter stands for a different digit. *Find them.*

```
    L D C F L
            3
  ───────────
  H J D H H L
  ───────────
```

105 Uncle Bungle Moves to Addition

Uncle Bungle has now, I think, made the point that he can get a subtraction wrong, but he always likes to move to fresh fields and different sums, and he has just been showing that what he can do for subtraction he can also do for addition.

He has made up an addition sum in which all the figures are 1 wrong, that is 1 more or 1 less than the correct figure. It looks like this:

```
    6 3 2 3
    9 6 0 6
  ───────────
  2 3 2 5 6
  ───────────
```

Find the correct addition sum.

106 The Lie Drug

Football, Three Teams

Doctor Wotta-Woppa has had great success in producing a new, effective and particularly subtle lie drug. Effective because it works – so far at least – and all those who take it tell lies. Subtle because, as shown in the latest test, not only do those who use it produce figures that are wrong, but figures that are incorrect by the same amount – in this latest example by 1.

He used it on a friend of his who is particularly interested in football. This friend was asked to write down the figures of the number of matches played, won, lost, etc., of three local football teams, who were all going to play each other once. And he produced this:

	Played	Won	Lost	Drawn	Goals for	Goals against
A	1	0	1	0	4	2
B	2	1	0	1	2	2
C	2	1	1	0	3	1

Each figure was 1 out, that is to say it was 1 more or 1 less than the correct figure.

Find the score in each match.

107 Ring Us!

The telephone has at last come to the Island of Imperfection and everyone is madly ringing everybody else. They have not yet discovered the fun of wrong numbers, though, for the numbers are so small that there is not much possibility of error.

There are three tribes on the Island – the Pukkas, who always tell the truth, the Wotta-Woppas, who never tell the truth, and the Shilli-Shallas, who make statements which are alternately true and false or false and true.

This story is about a conversation between three people – A, B and C – one from each tribe.

They speak as follows:

A: (1) 'C's number is greater than 15.'
   (2) 'B's number is 13.'
B: (1) 'C's number is halfway between A's and B's.'
   (2) 'C is a Pukka.'
C: (1) 'A is a Shilli-Shalla.'
   (2) 'C's number is less than 15.'

Their telephone numbers are all between 10 and 20 inclusive.

Find the tribes to which they belong. What can you say about their telephone numbers?

There are no 0's.

Across

1 The square of an odd number
3 Half 1 Down
4 The same when reversed

Down

1 Twice 3 Across
2 Digits all go up or all go down
The difference between the first and second digits is the
same as the difference between the second and third

109 Addition

Letters for Digits, Two Numbers

In the addition sum below the digits have been replaced by letters. The same letter stands for the same digit wherever it appears, and different letters stand for different digits.

```
    Y A B A E W T P
    Y A W H P T T H
  -----------------
  J P K P J E Y A H
```

Write out the sum with numbers substituted for letters.

110 Division

Some Missing Figures

A division sum.

```
              - 7 -
  - -) - - - - 1
      - - 4
      -------
        - - -
        - -
      -------
          - -
          - -
          -----
```

Find the missing digits.

124

111 Right or Wrong?

I was rather pleased with the latest puzzle which I had made up about the five workers in our factory having a competition, and I hastened to show it to a friend of mine.

It went like this:

'Alf, Bert, Charlie, Duggie and Ernie made statements about their order in a competition they were having. They spoke as follows:

A: "Charlie was higher than I was."

B: "I was second or third."

C: "Duggie was higher than Ernie."

D: "I was fourth or fifth."

E: "Alf was higher than Bert."'

I was surprised however to see how quickly my friend claimed to have done it.

When I looked at my notes however his answer did not agree with mine – and then, suddenly, I saw the light. 'Oh, by the way,' I said, 'I forgot to tell you that all those statements are wrong.'

What was the order my friend got, assuming that all the statements were true? And what was the order he would have got assuming that they were all false?

112 Football

Four Teams, Old Method

Four football teams – A, B, C and D – are all to play each other once. After some of the matches have been played a table giving some details of the matches played, won, lost, etc., looked like this:

	Played	Won	Lost	Drawn	Goals for	Goals against
A	2					
B				2	5	5
C	2		1		3	1
D				1		2

Find the score in each match.

113 Cricket

Three Teams

A, B and C have all played each other once at cricket.

Points are awarded as follows:

to the side that wins, 10;

to the side that wins on the first innings in a drawn match, 6;

to the side that loses on the first innings in a drawn match, 2;

to each side for a tie, 5;

to each side for a tie on the first innings in a drawn match, 4;

to the side that loses, 0.

A, B and C got 12, 6 and 10 points respectively.

Find the result of each match.

114 Letters for Digits

A Multiplication

In the multiplication sum below letters have been substituted for digits. The same letter stands for the same digit wherever it appears, and different letters stand for different digits.

$$
\begin{array}{r}
W\,V\,G\,E \\
W \\
\hline
T\,F\,E\,W \\
\hline
\end{array}
$$

You are told that W is an odd number and that there are no 0's.

Find the digits for which the letters stand.

115 C was Silent

There are three tribes on the Island of Imperfection, the Pukkas, who always tell the truth, the Wotta-Woppas, who never tell the truth, and the Shilli-Shallas, who make statements which are alternately true and false or false and true.

A, B, C and D are inhabitants of the island. Two of them are Pukkas, one is a Wotta-Woppa and the fourth is a Shilli-Shalla.

A, B and D make statements as follows:

A: 'C is more truthful than D.'

B: 'D is a Pukka.'

D: 'A is a Pukka.'

Find the tribes to which A, B, C and D belong.

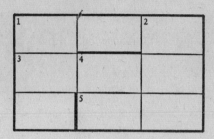

There are no 0's

Across

1 The sum of the digits is 11
3 Each digit is 2 greater than the one before
5 A perfect square

Down

1 The same when reversed
2 An even number. Each digit is less than the one before
4 An even number, and a multiple of 11

Letters for Digits, Three Numbers

In the following sum letters have been substituted for digits,
and three five-figure numbers have been added together. The
same letter stands for the same digit wherever it appears, and
different letters stand for different digits.

```
      Y R R M P
      Y R P M P
      Y R Y M P
    _____
    R Y M A B P
```

Write out the sum with numbers substituted for letters.

Sometimes he gets things right and sometimes he doesn't, but just at the moment I am afraid that Uncle Bungle seems to be passing through a bad patch. In the latest division sum which he has produced only four figures were given and to get one of them wrong seems to me an unusually high percentage. Not, mind you, that he can't do better than that, for there have been occasions when he has got all the figures wrong!

The division sum that he produced looked like this:

$$
\begin{array}{r}
\!- 2 \\
5 -) \overline{5\ -\ -\ -} \\
- -\ - \\
\overline{} \\
- - \\
- 9
\end{array}
$$

Which figure was wrong? What should the correct division sum have been?

119 Football

Four Teams, Old Method

A, B, C and D are each to play each other once at football. After some of the matches had been played a table giving some details of matches played, won, lost, drawn, etc., looked like this:

	Played	Won	Lost	Drawn	Goals for	Goals against	Points
A	2			1	0		
B							0
C	1						
D			0	0	4	2	4

2 points are given for a win, and 1 for a draw.

Find the score in each match.

120 The Older the Truer ★★

On the Island of Imperfection there are three tribes – the Pukkas, who always tell the truth, the Wotta-Woppas, who never tell the truth, and the Shilli-Shallas, who make statements which are alternately true and false or false and true.

This story deals with three members of the Island, one from each tribe, whom we shall call A, B and C.

They make statements as follows:

A: (1) 'B is 7 years older than me.'
    (2) 'B is not more than 26.'
B: (1) 'The Shilli-Shalla is 6 years older than the Wotta-Woppa.'
    (2) 'I am older than C.'
C: (1) 'A is a Pukka.'
    (2) 'A is 5 years older than B.'

It was interesting to notice that the older a man was the more truthful was his tribe.

You are told that B's second remark was true, and that their ages are between 19 and 31 inclusive, and that they are all different.

What can you say about the ages and the tribes of A, B and C?

133

Three-Star Puzzles

121 Two of One, and One of the Other Two

The inhabitants of the Island of Imperfection are very friendly and often go about in threes – one from each tribe. But this time, for a change, there were two of one tribe, and one from each of the other two. But I had better explain.

There are three tribes on the island – the Pukkas, who always tell the truth, the Wotta-Woppas, who never tell the truth, and the Shilli-Shallas, who make statements which are alternately true and false or false and true.

The four inhabitants – A, B, C and D – speak as follows:

A: 'D is a Pukka.'
B: 'A is a Pukka.'
C: 'I belong to a less truthful tribe than A does.'
D: 'B is a Wotta-Woppa.'

Find the tribes to which A, B, C and D belong.

122 Multiply by 5

In the following multiplication by 5 each letter stands for a different digit. *Find them.*

```
      X Q R X F X A
                  5
      ─────────────
      A M Q K D F Q
      ─────────────
```

I have often thought that Uncle Bungle has much in common with the Ancient Mariner. He may not have a long grey beard, but he has certainly got 'glittering eyes'.

In his famous poem Coleridge describes how this character stopped 'one in three'. My uncle is certainly likely to do this when he gets the chance, with the same motives and in the same way as his better known predecessor. And I think that the Ancient Mariner would be quite likely to get his sums wrong.

But be that as it may, in his latest long division sum my Uncle has managed to get one of the three figures given wrong. And what is left looks like this:

```
        7 -
- 5)- - -
     - -
     - - -
     - - 8
```

Which figure is wrong? Find the correct division sum.

138

1		2		3	
4					
////	////	5			

There are no 0's.

Across

1 A perfect square
4 The same when reversed
5 Even. Sum of digits is 11

Down

1 A perfect square
2 Sum of digits is 16
3 Each digit is 2 greater than the digit before

Letters for Digits, Two Numbers

Below is an addition sum with letters substituted for digits. The same letter stands for the same digit wherever it appears, and different letters stand for different digits.

```
X J D F C
C D F C C
─────────
J J J Y J
```

Write out the sum with numbers substituted for letters.

Alf, Bert, Charlie, Duggie, Ernie and Fred have been having a competition again, but this time it was a very nice simple one. They were running 100 metres for a small prize given by the Managing Director, and I am glad to say that there were no ties as this might have complicated the issue.

You might be interested to hear something about the results.

Charlie was as many places behind Fred as Bert was before Alf, but the difference between Charlie and Fred was more than one.

Bert was not first, and Fred was not fourth, and neither Alf nor Charlie was last. The number of Duggie's place was half the number of Ernie's.

In what order did the six of them come in the 100-metre race?

127 Football

Five Teams, Old Method

Five football teams, A, B, C, D and E, are to play each other once. After some of the matches have been played a table giving some details of matches played, won, lost, etc., looked like this:

	Played	Won	Lost	Drawn	Goals for	Goals against
A			1	0	1	2
B			1			5
C	2		1		7	4
D		1		0	2	2
E		2		0	5	2

Find the score in each match.

142

128 Some More Wrong Additions

Not many people can add wrong, or for that matter do anything wrong, as well as Uncle Bungle. But only 1 out, he says proudly, as though a little mistake like this doesn't really matter very much.

Some of us, however, like to get things right. So let us see if we can find the correct numbers which have been added together, by looking at the incorrect figures in the addition which Uncle Bungle has given me (only 1 out remember).

His addition sum (if that is what you can call it) looks like this:

$$\begin{array}{r} 7\ 6\ 6\ 8 \\ 2\ 6\ 9\ 2 \\ \hline 9\ 0\ 2\ 7 \end{array}$$

Find the figures in the correct addition sum.

Letters for Digits

In the following division sum each letter stands for a different digit.

```
            k n m d
  h e ) e n d j n
        c g
        ─────
        k d
        d k
        ─────
          p j
          g m
          ─────
            m n
            m h
            ─────
              h
```

Find the sum with the letters replaced by digits.

130 Cricket

Four Teams

Four teams – A, B, C and D – have each played each other once at cricket.

Points are given as follows:

to the side that wins, 10;
to the side that wins on the first innings in a drawn match, 6;
to the side that loses on the first innings in a drawn match, 2;
to each side for a tie, 5;
to the side that loses, 0.

A, B, C and D got 25, 2, 8 and 21 points respectively.

Find the result of each match.

131 Division

Some Missing Figures

A division sum.

```
           - - -
- -)- - - - 5
    - 0
    - - -
    4 - -
        - -
        - -
```

Find the missing digits.

Letters for Digits, Three Numbers

In the addition sum below the digits have been replaced by letters. The same letter stands for the same digit wherever it appears, and different letters stand for different digits.

```
G G J D G F F
G G G P B F F
G G B D G F F
─────────────
Z N Y H P B G
```

Write out the sum with numbers substituted for letters.

133 A Cross Number

1	2	/////
3		4
5		

There are no 0's.

Across

1 A factor of 5 Across
3 Even
5 The square of 4 Down.

Down

1 Sum of digits is 15
2 Each digit is 2 greater than the digit before
4 The second digit is greater than the first

134 Football

Four Teams, New Method

Goals are what the public goes to see, and goals are what they have been enjoying as a result of the new football method.

In this method 10 points are awarded for a win, 5 points for a draw, and 1 point for each goal scored whatever the result of the game.

A, B, C and D are eventually going to play each other once. After all but two of the matches had been played, the situation was as follows:

A – 7 points
B – 8 points
C – 39 points
D – 3 points

Each side scored at least 1 goal in every match, but not more than 7 goals were scored in any game.

Find the scores in all the matches.

135 Doors, Doors, Doors ★★★

The workers in our factory, all seven of them, have been having a holiday on the Island of Imperfection. There are three tribes on the island, the Pukkas, who always tell the truth, the Wotta-Woppas, who never tell the truth, and the Shilli-Shallas, who make statements which are alternately true and false or false and true.

The authorities insisted that they should all join one of the three tribes and it so happens that Alf, Bert and Charlie have been accepted by different tribes for the duration of their stay.

Some people might say, in fact some people have said, that we are rather too keen on doors in our factory. And I suppose that there is something in what they say because, after all, of our seven employees three of them – the Door-Opener, the Door-Shutter and the Door-Knob-Polisher, are exclusively concerned with doors. And it so happens that these are the jobs which Alf, Bert and Charlie had before this holiday, although not necessarily in that order.

Alf, Bert and Charlie speak as follows:

A: (1) 'Charlie is more truthful than Bert.'
    (2) 'I am the Door-Shutter.'
B: (1) 'The Door-Shutter is a Wotta-Woppa.'
C: (1) 'Bert is a Pukka.'
    (2) 'I am not the Door-Opener.'

Find the tribes to which Alf, Bert and Charlie belong and the jobs which they had before they came to the island.

Letters for Digits

In the following division sum each letter stands for a different digit.

```
              b q g
        h v ) g h q h
              p b
              ─────
              p q
              m q
              ─────
              h e h
              v p g
              ─────
                v q
```

Find the sum with the letters replaced by digits.

137 Our Factory – Logic and Charm

It has always been my principle that if the workers in my factory are going to compete (and compete they certainly do), then they should try to show their superiority in things that really matter.

When Alf told me that he and Bert, Charlie, Duggie and Ernie were going to have a test to produce an order of merit in logic and in charm, I made it clear that this idea met with the complete approval of the Managing Director.

After all, some people think that logic matters, and a great deal of charm may often be needed by my not very intelligent employees to persuade people that their particular brand of logic makes sense.

I was given some information about the order of merit in these two subjects, in which there were no ties.

As follows:

(1) Bert is as many places above Duggie in logic as Duggie is above Bert in charm. But neither Bert nor Duggie is first in either of them.

(2) Ernie is below Bert in charm and Bert is above Ernie in logic.

(3) Alf is less logical than Charlie, and Charlie is less charming than Alf.

(4) Ernie is neither the least logical nor the least charming.

Find their order of merit in logic and in charm.

138 Addition

Letters for Digits, Four Numbers

Below is an addition sum with letters substituted for digits. The same letter stands for the same digit wherever it appears, and different letters stand for different digits.

```
      P  P  R  P
      P  P  C  C
      P  R  R  P
      P  C  X  C
   ─────────────
   R  R  A  Q  R
```

Write out the sum with numbers substituted for letters.

139 Bungle Blunders

Bungle blunders once again.
'Which is wrong?' he cries in vain.
'Eight or six or five or two?'
That's a puzzle just for you.

```
           8 -
   - 2 ) - - 6
       - 5
       - -
       - -
```

One of the figures is wrong. Which one?

Find the correct division sum.

140 Half of them are Wotta-Woppas ★★★

There are three tribes on the Island of Imperfection, the Pukkas, who always tell the truth, the Wotta-Woppas, who never tell the truth, and the Shilli-Shallas, who make statements which are alternately true and false or false and true.

Some people rather disapprove of Wotta-Woppas, and for them it may be rather sad to see that in this latest puzzle half of the four people with whom we deal (whom we shall call A, B, C and D) are Wotta-Woppas, but of the other two one is a Pukka and the other is a Shilli-Shalla.

They make statements as follows:

A: 'B is a Pukka.'
B: 'A belongs to a more truthful tribe than D.'
C: 'D is a Wotta-Woppa.'
D: 'A is a Pukka.'

Find the tribes to which A, B, C and D belong.

141 Football

Four Teams, Old Method

Four football teams – A, B, C and D – are to play each other once. After some of the matches have been played a table giving some details of matches played, won, lost, etc., looked like this:

	Played	Won	Lost	Drawn	Goals for	Goals against
A		0		0	2	3
B				0		1
C	2				4	
D		0		1		5

Find the score in each match.

Figures All Wrong

In the following, obviously incorrect, division sum the pattern is correct, but all the figures are wrong.

```
              8 3
        9 2)7 0 2 6
            6 6 0
            ─────
            2 2 4
            1 0 2
            ─────
```

The correct division comes out exactly.

The digits in the answer (that is in the top line) are only 1 out, but all the other digits may be incorrect by any amount.

Find the correct figures.

143 Cricket

Five Teams

A, B, C, D and E are all to play each other once at cricket.
  Points are awarded as follows:
to the side that wins, 10;
to the side that wins on the first innings in a drawn match, 6;
to the side that loses on the first innings in a drawn match, 2;
to each side for a tie, 5;
to each side for a tie on the first innings in a drawn match, 4;
to the side that loses, 0.
  A, B, C, D and E got 6, 35, 11, 12 and 2 points respectively.
  You are told that A and C only played two matches, and
that D won one of theirs. C did not play E.

Find the result of each match.

144 Addition

Letters for Digits, Three Numbers

In the addition sum below the digits have been replaced by
letters. The same letter stands for the same digit wherever it
appears, and different letters stand for different digits.

```
  B Y T Z B X D D
  B S V Z D B D D
  B B S Z D B D D
  ─────────────────
  X V N P P N B B
```

Write out the sum with numbers substituted for letters.

145 What Done It?

Professor Knowall is prepared to investigate all sorts of mistakes or misdemeanours, not only 'Who Done It?' but also 'What Done It?', so I therefore asked him if he could help me investigate the trouble in my car.

There seemed to be three separate things that were going wrong, or rather made the car less satisfactory than the makers intended it should be.

It was all right when it was not running, but when the engine was on and I tried to get things to work, there was a high-pitched scream, a rumble and a dull thud.

I felt pretty certain that the causes of these things were one of the following: the windscreen wipers, opening the left-hand window, putting on the handbrake, pulling the button that said 'Push Heater' or opening the right-hand window.

But I did not see how to find out which caused which.

But, as I knew he would, the Professor was able to solve my little problem.

'What you want, my dear Serjeant Simple,' he said, 'is a controlled experiment.'

I must admit that I did not quite understand what he meant by this, but I knew that I could rely upon him to explain it and to do whatever was necessary. To cut a long story short the result of our controlled experiment was as follows:

When we opened the left-hand window, put on the handbrake, and also opened the right-hand window, the result was the high-pitched scream and the rumble.

The result of turning on the windscreen wipers, putting on the handbrake, pulling the 'Push Heater' button, and opening the right-hand window, was a rumble and a dull thud.

We then tried the windscreen wipers, together with the opening of the left-hand window, putting on the handbrake, and pulling the 'Push Heater' button. The result was the high-pitched scream and the dull thud.

Our last experiment was the windscreen wipers again, the opening of both the left-hand and the right-hand windows, and putting on the handbrake. We then had what one might describe as the complete orchestra, that is to say the high-pitched scream, the rumble and the dull thud.

It will not surprise my readers to hear that I did not quite know what to do with this evidence, but perhaps they will.

On the assumption that the three noises which we are investigating each have one single cause, find out what is responsible for the high-pitched scream, the rumble and the dull thud.

I think it was just a coincidence that the richer the three inhabitants of the Island of Imperfection were, the more they told the truth. At any rate I would like to think so.

There are three tribes on the Island – the Pukkas, who always tell the truth, the Wotta-Woppas, who never tell the truth, and the Shilli-Shallas, who make statements which are alternately true and false or false and true.

A, B and C, one of whom comes from each tribe, are having a conversation about their weekly wages. The islanders have only recently got around to using money and the currency of the island is a Hope. I happen to know from another source that all their wages are between 21 and 41 Hopes per week inclusive, and that each man receives an exact number of Hopes.

They make statements as follows:

A: (1) 'B's wages are two-thirds of C's.'
    (2) 'My wages are 4 Hopes less than C's.'

B: (1) 'A's wages are four-fifths of C's.'
    (2) 'C's wages are 4 Hopes more than A's.'

C: (1) 'B's wages are 3 Hopes less than A's.'
    (2) 'My wages are an even number of Hopes.'

Find the tribes to which A, B and C belong, and their weekly wages.

147 Uncle Bungle Multiplies ★★★

From getting addition and subtraction sums wrong it is only a short step to getting multiplication sums wrong. And Uncle Bungle has now taken this step.

I am glad to say however that he has had the sense not to overdo things and all the figures are only 1 out.

It looked like this:

$$
\begin{array}{r}
1\;6\;6\;3 \\
3 \\
\hline
2\;1\;3\;7\;9 \\
\end{array}
$$

Find the correct sum.

148 Football

Four Teams, New Method

The new method of rewarding goals scored in football goes from strength to strength, and the score looks very different from the 0–0 and 1–0 of the old days.

Under this method 10 points are awarded for a win, 5 points for a draw, and 1 point for each goal scored. In the latest competition each side scored at least 1 goal in every match and in a match that was drawn each side scored at least 2 goals.

Points were awarded as follows:

A – 7
B – 13
C – 20
D – 4

Not more than 6 goals were scored in any match.

Find the score in each match.

Letters for Digits, Three Numbers

Below is an addition sum with letters substituted for digits.
The same letter stands for the same digit wherever it appears,
and different letters stand for different digits.

```
L P B R R
T L S R R
S B R R R
─────────
R L M P L
```

Write out the sum with numbers substituted for letters.

150 The Shilli-Shallas Come into their Own

There are three tribes on the Island of Imperfection, the Pukkas, who always tell the truth, the Wotta-Woppas, who never tell the truth, and the Shilli-Shallas, who make statements which are alternately true and false or false and true.

People tend not to take much notice of the Shilli-Shallas for they are, after all, the great example for posterity of those who cannot make up their minds. But in the particular situation with which this story deals, they have, in a sense, come into their own.

A, B, C and D are four inhabitants of the island. One of them is a Pukka, another is a Wotta-Woppa, but two of them, and this gives their tribe more importance than they usually have, are Shilli-Shallas.

They make statements as follows:

A: 'C is a Shilli-Shalla.'
B: 'D belongs to a more truthful tribe than I do.'
C: 'D is not a Shilli-Shalla.'
D: 'A is a Pukka.'

Find the tribes to which A, B, C and D belong.

Hints

For puzzles ending in 1 (i.e., 1, 11, 21, 31 ... 141)

1	Think what 'I' must be.
11	What can you say about the last digit in 1 Down?
21	Suppose B's statement is true.
31	Consider C.
41	How many points did each side get for wins and draws?
51	What can you say about the third digit for 2 Down? Then look at 4 Across.
61	Start by finding 0.
71	Consider D.
81	How must the divisor start?
91	Find 0 and 1.
101	Suppose Belinda's second remark is true.
111	Put the facts down clearly.
121	Suppose B's statement is true.
131	Find how the divisor ends.
141	Look at A.

For puzzles ending in 2 (i.e., 2, 12, 22, 32 ... 142)

2	Look at B's games.
12	Start by looking at C.
22	What can you say about scores in C's matches?
32	What is y?
42	How does 3 Down end? What is first figure of 1 Across and 1 Down?
52	How many points did B and C get for wins and draws and for goals?
62	Start by finding what points each side got for wins or draws.
72	Get P and then R.
82	What is the number of points got from wins and draws?
92	Look at 1 Down and 4 Across.

102   Go for M.

112   Consider C.

122   Start by finding X.

132   Go for G.

142   Consider the second figure in the answer.

For puzzles ending in 3 (i.e., 3, 13, 23, 33 . . . 143)

3   What can you say about Charlie and his statement?

13   Start by considering Bert's and Charlie's places.

23   'Bert was twice as many places above Alf, as Duggie was below Charlie.' Set out the possibilities of this.

33   Consider how 4 Across starts.

43   Suppose C's statement is true.

53   Consider George's statement.

63   What can you say about places where they are *not*?

73   Set the information out neatly, and start from the fact that the Bottle-Washer was third.

83   Remember that from 'If p, then q' it does *not* follow that 'If q, then p'.

93   Look at the last line down.

103   Look for 1 and 2.

113   Consider the different ways in which A can have got their points.

123   Find two figures that cannot both be right. How can you find which is wrong?

133   Look at 5 Across, 4 Down and 3 Across.

143   Consider B's games and results.

For puzzles ending in 4 (i.e., 4, 14, 24, 34 . . . 144)

4   What can you say about M, and then P?

14   What follows from A's statement?

24   From the fact that the second figure in answer is 1, what can you say about the divisor?

34   Think of the possibilities for B.

44   What can you say about n?

54   Consider the last column, and move to the left.

64   Consider 5 Across and 2 Down.

74   What is D?

84   What can you say about Z?

94   How many matches did B play?

104   Look on the right, and find L.

114   Suppose that W is 5.

124   Look at 5 Across and 3 Down.

134   Start with C.

144   What can you say about B?

For puzzles ending in 5 (i.e., 5, 15, 25, 35 . . . 145)

5   What is B? What is F?

15   What can you say about M?

25   Find P and then X.

35   Suppose C's statement is true.

45   Investigate the possibilities for L.

55   Get U and then T.

65   Consider how A can have got their points.

75   Consider what p, for example, is *not* caused by.

85   Look at 4 Down and 3 Across.

95   Go for P.

105   Consider figures on the right and then move to the left.

115   Suppose B's statement is true.

125   Look at the last and first columns.

135   Suppose C(1) true.

145   Remember that each noise has a *single* cause.

For puzzles ending in 6 (i.e., 6, 16, 26, 36 . . . 146)

6   Draw a diagram showing their possible places.

16   Start by considering the first two digits in the answer.

26   Who did C play?

36   Who was A's drawn match against? What was the score?

46   Who did C play?

56   Look at the 3 in the answer. How must the divisor start?

66   The divisor times 5 contains two figures. What can you say about the divisor?

76   Look for mistakes. Two figures will be involved. How do you find which is wrong?

86   With the help of the 3 in the answer, think what the divisor must be.

96   Suppose A(2) is true.

106 No team can play more than two matches. Therefore find figures for played, won, lost, drawn.

116 Consider 5 Across. Remember that 4 Down and 2 Down are both even.

126 Set out possibilities neatly.

136 Try to find 0 and 1.

146 Suppose B(2) is true.

For puzzles ending in 7 (i.e., 7, 17, 27, 37 . . . 147)

7   What were the scores in A's two games?

17   Consider B.

27   Consider the possibilities for 1 Across.

37   Look at 3 and second 8. What can you say about the divisor?

47   Draw a diagram with names down and jobs across.

57   What can you say about A v. C?

67   Think what you can say about B.

77   Compare A's and B's goals for, with C's goals against. What can you say about scores in A v. B?

87   Go for Alf's position.

97   There is no way of getting certain points. Which?

107 Suppose that B(2) is true.

117 Go for P and R.

127 What can you say about B's matches?

137 Set out the possibilities for logic and charm. What can you say about who was first?

147 Think what 9 must be.

For puzzles ending in 8 (i.e., 8, 18, 28, 38 . . . 148)

8 What can you say about the first figure in the answer?

18 Consider 2 Down and 1 Across.

28 What can you say about B's statement?

38 Think who was there when there was *no* pencil stealing, etc.

48 What follows from the fact that B's first statement is true?

58 Consider A's statement.

68 Think about C on the second Saturday.

78 Consider 3 Across and 4 Down.

88 What can you say about B's results?

98 How must the divisor start?

108 Consider 3 Across and 1 Down.

118 Look for two figures that cannot both be right. And then look for two more figures that cannot both be right.

128 Work from right to left.

138 Go for R.

148 Think how the points must be divided between wins and draws on the one hand and goals on the other.

For puzzles ending in 9 (i.e., 9, 19, 29, 39 . . . 149)

9 Think what follows from the fact that Clever and Loopy are liars.

19 How can A have got their points?

29 Consider the possibilities for A's points.

39 Start by considering the last line down and then move to the left.

49 Think what you can say about the divisor.

59 Start by trying to find M.

69 Suppose E was second.

79 Find M and then E.

89 Think of the possibilities for M and B in last column.

99 Consider 3 Down, and 1 Across and 4 Across.

109   Go for J and P.

119   Consider the drawn matches.

129   Try to find how the divisor starts.

139   Find two figures that cannot both be right. And then two more figures that cannot both be right.

149   Go for R.

For puzzles ending in 0 (i.e., 10, 20, 30, 40 . . . 150)

10   What can you say about Y?

20   Suppose A = 2.

30   Notice the fact that M and B add up to less than 10.

40   Remembering that there are no 1's; look at the first line down.

50   What is R?

60   Find M and then S.

70   What follows from the fact that B's first statement was false.

80   Draw up a table setting out the possibilities.

90   Think what follows from the fact that 'C does have not A on his right'.

100   What can you say about C?

110   The 7 in the answer should tell you quite a lot about the divisor.

120   We know that B(2) is true. Suppose that C(1) is also true.

130   Find the number of points for wins and draws.

140   Suppose B's statement is true.

150   What follows if we assume that B's statement is true?

Suggestions

Football, Old Method

The method of setting out a football table is best explained by looking at a simple situation in which A and B play each other once only.

Thus: (i)

	Played	Won	Lost	Drawn	Goals for	Goals against
A	1	1	0	0	4	2
B	1	0	1	0	2	4

It is easy to see that A beat B by 4–2. But all this information was not needed. We could have had:

(ii)

	Played	Won	Lost	Drawn	Goals for	Goals against
A	1					2
B	1					4

And we would have reached the same conclusion.

Suppose we have three teams, A, B and C, who have played each other once (so that there are three games). Then the complete information might be:

(iii)

	Played	Won	Lost	Drawn	Goals for	Goals against
A	2	0	1	1	3	4
B	2	2	0	0	2	0
C	2	0	1	1	3	4

But a lot of this information is not needed. If B scored only 2 goals and won both their two matches, the score in each must have been 1–0. So B v. A and B v. C were both 1–0. And since the third match (A v. C) was drawn and A scored 3 goals, A v. C must have been 3–3 (remember that A scored no goals against B).

Much less information was therefore needed. In fact the following would have been sufficient:

(iv)

	Played	Won	Lost	Drawn	Goals for	Goals against
A					3	
B		2			2	
C				1		

(And this is Puzzle No. 2.)

But in solving this puzzle although it might be helpful to fill up the above diagram, a table that the solver is likely to find more helpful would be this:

172

(v)

	A	B	C
A	✕		
B		✕	
C			✕

Reading across this gives us the results of A's games against B and against C from A's point of view. And since A did not play A, that square is marked with a cross (as is B v. B and C v. C).

We know that B won both their matches and that the score must therefore have been 1–0 in each. We can fill this up in B's line across. And if B v. A was 1–0, then A v. B was 0–1, etc.

So we have:

(vi)

	A	B	C
A	✕	0–1	
B	1–0	✕	1–0
C		0–1	✕

And since A scored 3 goals, and since C drew a match (which must have been against A), A v. C was 3–3 (as was C v. A).

When more teams are concerned it may not be so easy to find a starting-point. A harder (but not really very hard) example may help.

Puzzle No. 127 on page 142.

(vii)

	Played	Won	Lost	Drawn	Goals for	Goals against
A			1	0	1	2
B			1			5
C	2		1		7	4
D		1		0	2	2
E		2		0	5	2

The total of 'goals for' must equal the total of 'goals against' (for each goal appears twice, as a goal for and a goal against).

∴ B's goals for was 0 (to make goals for and goals against both 15). ∴ B (with no goals) cannot have won a match.

Neither A, D or E drew a match, and C cannot have drawn the second of their two matches, for that would make the total of their goals against greater than their goals for (whereas in fact it was 7–4). ∴ no match was drawn. ∴ B can only have played one match, and the score was 0–5.

And if we look at B's goals against we see that B's only match must have been against C. (A and D did not score enough goals and though E scored 5 goals, at least one of them must have been in the other of the two matches which they won.)

∴ B v. C was 0–5, and we know that C's other match was 2–4.

174

This makes a good starting-point. A diagram like (v) (but for five teams) will now help.

Football, New Method

In this method 10 points are given for a win, 5 points to each side in a match that is drawn, and 1 point for each goal scored. ∴ if A plays B and C, and the scores in those matches were 3–2 and 3–3, then A's points would be: 10+5+6 (for goals scored), i.e. 21. And B's points (for one game) would be: 0+2 (for goals scored) i.e. 2; and C's points would be 5+3, i.e. 8.

Let us consider Puzzle No 41, between three teams – A, B and C.

The total number of points are A, 9; B, 26; C, 7. And we are told that the teams have played each other once. (And that each team has scored at least 1 goal in every match.)

Three matches were played, ∴ 30 points were awarded for wins and draws. ∴ B got 20 points (no team can have got more, for only two matches were played by each team).

∴ A and C each got 5 points for a draw (there is one more match to be played, and this is the only possibility). ∴ numbers of points for goals are: A, 4; B, 6; C, 2. C must have scored 1 goal in each match. ∴ C v. A was 1–1; and C v. B was 1–?. ∴ A got 3 goals in their other match (against B), ∴ A v. B was 3–?.

We know that B won both their matches and scored only 6 goals.

∴ B v. C must have been 2–1
and B v. A must have been 4–3.

The complete solution is   A v. B   3–4;
                                 A v. C   1–1;
                                 B v. C   2–1.

Letters for Digits

Look at a simple addition sum in which letters have been substituted for digits. The same letter stands for the same digit wherever it appears, and different letters stand for different digits.

Suppose we had:

```
    (a) (b) (c)
         R   R
         R   T
    ───────────
     X   X   X
```

The most that can be carried when 2 digits are added together is 1. $\therefore X = 1$.

From (b) $R = 5$ ($5 + 5 = 10$, and there must be 1 to carry to make 11).

$\therefore T = 6$ ($5 + 6 = 11$).

Suppose now that we had:

```
    (a) (b) (c) (d) (e)
         R   R   P   T
         R   T   P   C
    ───────────────────
     X   X   X   T   Z
```

The argument we have already used still applies to:

```
     R   R
     R   T
    ───────
 X   X   X
```

(There cannot be 1 to carry from (d), for if there were T would be 5, but we know that $R = 5$.)

$\therefore$ we know that $X = 1$, $R = 5$ and $T = 6$. And knowing that $T = 6$, we can see from (d) that $P = 3$. And since there is nothing to carry from (e) and $T = 6$, $\therefore$ C must be 2 and Z must be 8. (1 and 3 are X and P.)

$\therefore$ Complete solution is:

$$
\begin{array}{r}
5\ 5\ 3\ 6 \\
5\ 6\ 3\ 2 \\
\hline
1\ 1\ 1\ 6\ 8
\end{array}
$$

An important point that arises from this is that the discovery of some letters is likely to make it easier to find out more. The fact that C was 2 and X was 8 was found to some extent by elimination.

Long Division

There are several different kinds of long division sums in this book. It may be helpful therefore if we say something about:

1. an ordinary long division sum;
2. long division sum with letters substituted for digits;
3. long division sums with most of the figures missing, and in some cases with one of the figures wrong;
4. long division sums with all the figures wrong.

1 Ordinary long division

(i) Let's start with a 'short' division sum. Suppose that we are going to divide 2308 by 3. The work might be set out like this:

$$
3\,)\,2\ 3\ 0\ 8
$$

$$
7\ 6\ 9 + \text{a remainder of } 1.
$$

In doing this some of the work has been done mentally. We said '3 into 2 will not go; 3 into 23 goes 7 times, and there is a remainder of 2; 3 into 20 goes 6 times and there is a remainder of 2; 3 into 28 goes 9 times and there is a remainder of 1.'

We might have expressed this in more detail by making a long division sum of it thus:

```
        7 6 9
3 ) 2 3 0 8
    2 1
    ———
      2 0
      1 8
      ———
        2 8
        2 7
        ———
          1
```

This is just the same as what we did above, except that it is put down in more detail – especially the remainders. The number of times that 3 goes into 2308 is 769, and there is a remainder of 1.

(ii) Let us consider now a long division sum in which we divide by 17.

Thus:

```
          2 3
1 7 ) 4 0 3
      3 4
      ———
        6 3
        5 1
        ———
        1 2
```

The method can be seen to be the same as when we were dividing by 3. The result is 23 and there is a remainder of 12.

2 Long division in which letters have been substituted for digits.

Thus:

$$
\begin{array}{r}
\,\text{g b m} \quad (a) \\
\hline
\text{h g})\overline{\text{h h b g}} \quad (b) \\
\,\text{h g} \quad\;\; (c) \\
\hline
\,\text{g b g} \quad (d) \\
\,\text{r m} \quad\;\; (e) \\
\hline
\,\text{g p} \quad\;\; (f) \\
\end{array}
$$

In this sum the same letter stands for the same digit wherever it appears. And if we find that, for example, r = 9, then we know that nothing else can be 9.

A starting-point can be got from the fact that (hg) (c) is the same as the divisor, ∴ g (the first digit in (a)) is 1. (We could also have got this from the fact that since (d) is a three-figure number, and (e) is only a two-figure number, then g = 1.)

From (b), (c) and (d) since g = 1, h = 2 (h−g = g). And since two figures have been brought down in (d), b (the second figure in (a)) is 0. So we have:

$$
\begin{array}{r}
\,1\;0\;- \quad (a) \\
\hline
2\;1)\overline{2\;2\;0\;1} \quad (b) \\
\,2\;1 \quad\;\; (c) \\
\hline
\,1\;0\;1 \quad (d) \\
\,-\;- \quad\;\; (e) \\
\hline
\,1\;- \quad\;\; (f) \\
\end{array}
$$

21 goes into 101 (d) 4 times. ∴ (e) is 84 and (f) is 17.
∴ r = 8, m = 4 and p = 7.

And complete solution is:

$$
\begin{array}{r}
1\;0\;4 \\
21\overline{)2\;2\;0\;1} \\
2\;1 \\
\hline
1\;0\;1 \\
\;\;8\;4 \\
\hline
\;\;1\;7
\end{array}
$$

3 Long division sums with most figures missing
(i)

$$
\begin{array}{r}
-\;- \qquad (a) \\
-\;-\overline{)-\;-\;-\;2} \qquad (b) \\
-\;3 \qquad (c) \\
\hline
-\;- \qquad (d) \\
-\;- \qquad (e) \\
\hline
1\;- \qquad (f)
\end{array}
$$

In this long division sum a blank (–) indicates that there is a
figure there, but we do not know what it is. We know, for
example, that we are dividing a four-figure number ending in
2 (b), by a two-figure number. This puzzle (like a lot of the
others) is very much easier than it looks at first sight.

When we subtract –3 (c) from the first three figures of (b)
we are left with a single figure (the first figure of (d)). Therefore (b) must start 10–, and (c) must be 93. (If we subtracted
93 from 110, there would be another figure at the beginning
of (d).) (e) cannot be 93, for there could not then be a 1 at
the beginning of (f).

∴ the divisor is a factor of 93. The only factors of 93 are 31 and
3.

∴ divisor is 31.

(*b*) must start 102 or less, for otherwise there would be another figure in (*d*).

∴ (*d*) must start with 9, 8 or 7. ∴ (*e*) must be 31 times 2, i.e. 62. ∴ (*d*) is 72, (*e*) is 62, and (*f*) is 10.

Complete solution

```
           3 2
    3 1 ) 1 0 0 2
           9 3
           ‾‾‾
           7 2
           6 2
           ‾‾‾
           1 0
           ‾‾‾
```

(ii) A long division sum with most of the figures missing and with one of the figures wrong:

```
           7 –      (a)
   – 5 ) – – –      (b)
         – –        (c)
         ‾‾‾
       – – –        (d)
       – – 8        (e)
       ‾‾‾‾
```

In this long division sum (Puzzle No. 123) you are told that one of the three figures given is wrong. And the question is: 'Which figure is wrong? Find the correct division sum.' In this example it is not possible to point to a certain figure by itself and say 'This one must be wrong.' We must start by trying to find a disagreement between two figures, a situation in which they cannot both be right.

Since the divisor is –5, every multiple of it must end in 0 or in 5. ∴ either the 5 in the divisor or the 8 in (e) must be wrong.

And if the divisor is –5, it must be at least 15. And 15 times 7 (the first figure in (*a*)) is 105. This has three figures, but

181

(*c*) has only two. ∴ either the 5 in the divisor or the 7 in (*a*) must be wrong.

But since we know that only one figure is wrong, it must be the 5 in the divisor. ∴ what we know about the correct sum is:

$$
\begin{array}{r}
7\; - \quad (a) \\
\hline
-\;-\,)\overline{-\;-\;-} \quad (b) \\
-\;- \quad (c) \\
\hline
-\;-\;- \quad (d) \\
-\;-\;8 \quad (e)
\end{array}
$$

Readers who have got as far as this would probably like to finish it off themselves. (The solution is on page 289.)

4 Long division sums with all the figures wrong

$$
\begin{array}{r}
2\;9 \quad (a) \\
8\;4\,)\overline{2\;2\;2\;3} \quad (b) \\
6\;2 \quad (c) \\
\hline
6\;9\;3 \quad (d) \\
4\;9\;3 \quad (e)
\end{array}
$$

The above example is Puzzle No. 49. We are told that all the figures are 1 out (i.e. 1 more or 1 less than the correct figures).

With the experience that the reader should now have, a few hints should be enough.

Thus: (*b*) can only start with 1; (*c*) cannot be less than the divisor, ∴ (*c*) must be 73, the divisor is 73, and the first figure in (*a*) is 1. The second figure in (*a*) can only be 8; 8 × 73 = 584; ∴ (*d*) and (*e*) are 584.

The Island of Imperfection

There are three tribes on this island. The Pukkas, who always tell the truth, the Wotta-Woppas, who never tell the truth, and the Shilli-Shallas, who make statements which are alternately true and false or false and true.

Some of the inhabitants make statements, and we are asked to find the tribes to which they belong, and various other things that may follow from their statements.

As always, the starting-point is likely to be the difficulty. It may often be helpful to start by supposing that a certain statement is true or false and then to think out what follows. But it will be very important to realize in this method that agreement is not likely to be very helpful. What we are looking for is disagreement or contradiction.

Consider Puzzle No. 28 on page 44.

Let us suppose that B's statement is true, so that A is a Pukka.

∴ all A's statements are true.

∴ A's statement that he is a Shilli-Shalla is true.

But this is impossible and contradicts our original assumption that B's statement was true.

∴ We can be quite certain that B's statement is not true.

∴ A is not a Pukka, and since B has made a false statement he is not a Pukka either.

∴ C is a Pukka (no one else can be).

∴ C's statement is true and B belongs to a less truthful tribe than A does. ∴ B must be a Wotta-Woppa, and A must be a Shilli-Shalla (the Wotta-Woppas are less truthful than the Shilli-Shallas).

This puzzle should give you a good idea of the method recommended for finding the tribes to which the various inhabitants of the island belong. Once these have been found and one knows which statements are true and which are false the rest of the puzzle is likely to be comparatively easy and no particular comments are needed.

Cross Numbers

In a cross-number puzzle it is unlikely that any clue will stand by itself, that is to say can be solved without reference to other clues. If we had a clue, for example: '7 times 9', that would be likely to make the puzzle too easy. We will usually find that each clue has to be considered with one, or perhaps two, or more, others.

Consider Puzzle No. 18 on page 34.

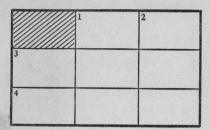

There are no 0's.

Across
1 A perfect square
3 The same when reversed; digits all even
4 Two of the digits are odd; and each one is at least 2 greater than the one before

Down
1 The sum of the digits is 15
2 The digits are all even; each one is greater than the one before
3 A multiple of 7

To find a starting-point may not be immediately easy. But if we look at 2 Down we can see that there are not many alternatives. It must start with either 2 or 4. And if we look at 1 Across ('A perfect square') we see that 2 Down cannot start with 2, for no perfect square ends in 2.

∴ 2 Down can only be 468.

And the only two-figure perfect square ending in 4 is 64. From 3 Across, 3 Down must start with 6, and can only be 63. And the reader will have no difficulty in seeing that 4 Across must be 358, and 1 Down is 645.

Again, as with so many of these puzzles, the difficulty is to find a starting-point. What we need to do is try to find a square where the possibilities are small when we consider the clues in one direction, and are even smaller – preferably only one – when we consider the clues in the other direction.

We have seen that there are only two possibilities for the first digit of 2 Down (2 or 4), and that only one of these (4) can be the second digit of 1 Across.

These considerations enable us to fill in 4 of the 8 squares, and the rest follows fairly easily.

Our Factory

Most of the puzzles about our factory involve finding an order of merit for Alf, Bert, Charlie, etc.

The most important advice to be given for this is *to be orderly* – to set out the alternatives in such a way that it is possible to see, perhaps, that place number 2 could only be filled by one or two of the people concerned.

Let us look at Puzzle No. 13 (a race between five people) on page 30.

We are told that: (i) D was three places above E;
(ii) C was not fifth;

(iii) B's and C's places add up to 8 (there are no ties).

What we know about C, D and E can be set out thus:

1	D		C
2	D		C
3			C
4		E	C
5		E	

And from the fact that B's and C's places add up to 8 we can say, with certainty, that B must be fifth and C must be third (there were no ties, so they cannot both be fourth, and we know that C cannot be fifth).

And since B is fifth, E is not fifth, and we can see from the diagram that E must be fourth (there is no other possibility).

∴ from (i) D is first, ∴ A is second (the only place left).

Cricket

The puzzles about cricket are unlikely to present much difficulty once one sees the fundamental principle that must be used. This principle is best illustrated by giving an example.

Look at Puzzle No. 19 on page 35.

A, B and C have been having a cricket competition in which they have all played against each other once.

Points are awarded as follows:

to the side that wins, 10 points;

to the side that wins on the first innings in a drawn match, 6 points;

to the side that loses on the first innings in a drawn match, 2 points;

to each side in a match that is tied, 5 points;

to each side in an uncompleted match, that is tied on the first innings, 4 points;

to the side that loses, 0.

A got 7 points; B got 6 points; and C got 15 points.
Find the result of each match.

What we want to do, if possible, is to find a team that could only have got their points in one way. A got 7 points and there is no way of getting 7 points from two matches (and each team only played two matches) except by tying a match (5 points) and by losing a match on the first innings (2 points). This therefore is what A must have done.

B who got 6 points could not have got 5 points from a tied match for there is no way of getting one point. Therefore A's tied match must have been against C, and the match that A lost on the first innings must have been against B, who therefore got 6 points from it. B therefore got no points in their second match and they lost it against C, who got 10 points.

In some more complicated puzzles there may be one or more alternatives for the number of ways in which teams can have got their points. In this case it may be necessary to try the various possibilities. But we will find that only one of them is acceptable – that is to say fits the whole data of the problem.

Professor Knowall and Serjeant Simple

Puzzles about these two characters can usually be solved by remembering that the same cause has generally the same effect, but the same effect may be preceded by many different causes.

This is seen best in Puzzle No. 75, where the causes and effects are denoted by letters, which make it easier to see how they are related.

As the Professor says in this puzzle to Serjeant Simple: 'If I stand in the rain without any clothes I shall get wet'; and 'But I may also get wet in a lot of other ways, for example, by diving into the sea.'

We are told in this puzzle that there were six possible causes (A, B, C, D, E, F) and that they were followed by four possible defects in a certain machine. We are told that there was every reason to believe that each effect had just one single cause.

The details were as follows:

A, C, F were followed by q and r;
B, C, D, F were followed by s and r;
B, D, E were followed by p and s;
A, D, E, F were followed by p and q.

You are asked to find the causes of p, q, r and s.

What we need to do is to consider what could *not* have caused p. So we want to look at the situations where p is not present on the right.

We see that p is not present on the right in the first two of the four lines above. ∴ p cannot have been caused by A, B, C, D or F. (For if it were p would have been present when A, B, C, D or F were present.)

∴ p can only be caused by E.

Similarly when we consider q we can see that q was not caused by B, C, D, E or F. ∴ q was caused by A.

And the reader will find it easy now to see that r must have been caused by C, and that s must have been caused by B.

The same principle applies to most of the puzzles about the Professor and the Serjeant.

Solutions

1 Uncle Bungle is Stung by a Couple of Bees

```
    (a) (b) (c)
             I
         B   B
        ─────────
     I   L   L
```

In column (a) I must be 1 (there can never be more than 1 to carry when two digits are added together).

∴ the letter I = 1.

The first figure in (b) B must be 9, for otherwise there could not be three figures in the answer.

∴ L = 0 (1+9 = 10).

Complete solution

```
        1
      9 9
    ───────
  1 0 0
```

2 Football

Three Teams, Old Method

Consider B. They won two, and scored 2 goals.

∴ B v. A and B v. C were both 1–0.

A scored no goals against B, ∴ all 3 of A's goals were against C.

And since C drew one of their matches, C v. A was 3–3.

Complete solution
    A v. B 0–1
    A v. C 3–3
    B v. C 1–0

3 Duggie was Dumb

Since we are told that B's statement was false, C is a Pukka.
∴ C's statement is true and B is not a Shilli-Shalla.
∴ B is a Wotta-Woppa, and ∴ D must be a Shilli-Shalla.

Complete solution
    Bert is a Wotta-Woppa;
    Charlie is a Pukka;
    Duggie is a Shilli-Shalla.

4 Multiply by Two ★

If a digit (i.e. a number between 0 and 9) is multiplied by 2, the
most that can be carried is 1. ∴ M = 1.
∴ P = 2 (M×2);
∴ A = 4; ∴ X = 7 (7×2 = 14).

Complete solution
$$\begin{array}{r} 7\ 2\ 1 \\ 2 \\ \hline 1\ 4\ 4\ 2 \end{array}$$

5 Addition

Letters for Digits, Two Numbers

```
(a) (b) (c) (d)
     F   C   F
     F   C   B
  ─────────────
  B  B   J   C
```

From (a) B must be 1, for this is the most that can be carried when two digits are added together. ∴ B = 1.
∴ from (b) F = 5. And from (d) C = 5+1 = 6.
∴ in (c) J = 2.

Complete solution

```
    5 6 5
    5 6 1
  ─────────
  1 1 2 6
```

6 Competition in Our Factory

B was not first or third, ∴ he was second or fourth, thus:

```
1
2  B
3
4  B
```

D was two places below B.
∴ B must have been second and D fourth, thus:

```
1
2  B
3
4  D
```

And since C was two places above A, C was first and A third.

Complete solution
1 Charlie
2 Bert
3 Alf
4 Duggie

7 Football

Three Teams, Old Method

A did not draw any matches, but had as many goals for as against, ∴ they won one (1–0), and lost one (0–1).
B won both their matches, ∴ A v. B was 0–1, and A v. C was 1–0.
B scored 5 goals, 1 against A, ∴ 4 against C.
C scored 2 goals, 0 against A, ∴ 2 against B.
∴ B v. C was 4–2.

Complete solution
A v. B   0–1
A v. C   1–0
B v. C   4–2

8 Division

Letters for Digits

```
            d y     (a)                    - -
      d r ) r r m   (b)              - - ) - - -
            d r     (c)                    - -
          -------                        -----
          d p m     (d)                  - - -
          d p m     (e)                  - - -

          -------                        -----
```

(The reader is advised to draw a diagram, like the one on the right above, and to fill in the digits as they are discovered.)

Since (c) is the divisor, the first figure in (a) is 1. ∴ d = 1.

Consider (b), (c) and (d). Since r − r = p, ∴ p = 0.

And since r − d = d (we know that 1 has not been borrowed, and that d = 1), ∴ r = 2. ∴ divisor is 12.

12 × 8 = 96, ∴ to get the three figures in (d) and (e) we must multiply 12 by 9, and we get 108. ∴ m = 8, and y = 9.

Complete solution

```
            1 9
      1 2 ) 2 2 8
            1 2
          -------
            1 0 8
            1 0 8

          -------
```

194

9 Who Pinched My Bike ? ★

Clever's and Loopy's remarks are both false, ∴ neither Loopy nor Clever did it.

'Idle said that Loopy had told him that Noddy did it', but we know that Loopy was a liar, ∴ Noddy did not do it.

∴ Idle must have done it.

Complete solution

Idle pinched my bike.

10 Addition ★

Letters for Digits, Two Numbers

	(a)	(b)	(c)
	P	Y	X
	P	Y	X
	Y	Y	P

Consider (b). Remembering that not more than 1 can be carried, Y must be 9. (If Y was 8, we would have $8+8=7$ (at most), for $8+8=16$, and $16+1=17$.) ∴ from (a) P = 4, and from (c) X = 7. (Remember that 1 is to be carried to (b).)

Complete solution

```
  4 9 7
  4 9 7
  -----
  9 9 4
```

11 A Cross Number

1 Down is even.

∴ the first figure of 5 Across is even.

∴ 5 Across must be 258. (Think what would happen if it started with 4.)

∴ 1 Down is 642.

∴ 1 Across is 66.

∴ 2 Down is 685 and 3 Across is 489.

Complete solution

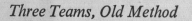

1 6	2 6	
3 4	8	4 9
5 2	5	8

12 Football ★

Three Teams, Old Method

Consider C. Since they lost none, and they had the same number of goals for as against, they won none.

But A drew none, ∴ C can only have drawn against B. And the score in this match was 4–4. ∴ only one other match was played (A v. B).

This was A's only match and they scored 3 goals. B scored 4 goals against C, and therefore they must have scored 1 against A (5 altogether).

Complete solution
    A v. B   3–1
    B v. C   4–4

13 Where was Alf?

From the facts that D is three places above E and that C is not last, we have as possibilities:

1	D	C
2	D	C
3		C
4	E	C
5	E	

B's and C's places add up to 8. There are no ties. ∴ B must be fifth and C third. And as E cannot be fifth, E is fourth, and D is first. ∴ A is second.

Complete solution
    1   Duggie
    2   Alf
    3   Charlie
    4   Ernie
    5   Bert

14 No Caps Now

Consider A's statement. It cannot be true for Wotta-Woppas never tell the truth. ∴ it is false.

∴ A is not a Wotta-Woppa, and he cannot be a Pukka for he has made a false statement. ∴ A is a Shilli-Shalla.

∴ C's statement is false.

∴ C is a Wotta-Woppa and B is a Pukka.

Complete solution
   A is a Shilli-Shalla;
   B is a Pukka;
   C is a Wotta-Woppa.

15 Addition

Letters for Digits, Two Numbers

$$
\begin{array}{ccc}
(a) & (b) & (c) \\
X & M & A \\
X & X & A \\
\hline
M & X & X
\end{array}
$$

Consider (b). Either $M = 0$ and there is nothing to carry from (c), or $M = 9$ and there is 1 to carry from (c).

But it is not possible for the first figure of the answer to be 0, ∴ $M = 9$. And from (a) $X = 4$. And since there is 1 to carry from (c), $A = 7$.

Complete solution

```
  4 9 7
  4 4 7
-------
  9 4 4
```

16 Not as it should be

```
(a) (b) (c)
     4   3
     5   7
  ---------
  2  0   7
```

When two digits are added together the most that can be carried is 1.

∴ the first figure of the answer is 1; and the second figure of the answer is also 1 (there is nothing else it can be).

Consider (c). If both figures (3 and 7) went up to 4 and 8, then the last figure of the answer would be 2, which is not possible. If one (either 3 or 7) went up and the other came down, the last figure of the answer would be 0, which again is not possible. ∴ both figures must come down and must become 2 and 6, and the last figure of the answer must be 8. And there is nothing to carry from (c). ∴ the first two figures of (b) can only be 5 and 6.

Complete solution

```
  5 2
  6 6
-------
1 1 8
```

17 Football

Three Teams, Old Method

B cannot have lost any, for they had no goals against, ∴ they only played one match and they won it (4–0). This match cannot have been against C, for they only had 3 goals against.
∴ B v. A was 4–0, and B did not play C.
∴ C only played A and the score was ?–3.
    A had 6 goals against, 4 scored by B and therefore 2 by C.
∴ A v. C was 3–2.

Complete solution
    A v. B   0–4
    A v. C   3–2

18 A Cross Number

Consider 2 Down. The first digit must be 2 or 4. But no perfect square ends in 2.
∴ 1 Across must be 64, and 2 Down must be 468.
∴ the first figure of 3 Across and of 3 Down is 6.
∴ 3 Down is 63.
∴ 4 Across is 358.
∴ 1 Down is 645.

	1 6	2 4
3 6	4	6
4 3	5	8

19 Cricket   ★

Three Teams

$$
\begin{array}{ll}
A & 7 \\
B & 6 \\
C & 15
\end{array}
$$

The only way of getting 7 points from two matches is by tying one (5 points) and by losing one on the first innings (2 points). ∴ this is what A must have done. B, with 6 points, could not have tied one (5 points) for there is no way of getting a single point. ∴ A v. C was a tie (5 points to each). ∴ A's match against B must have been a win for B on the first innings (6 points to B and 2 to A). And the third match (C v. B) was a win for C (10 points to C, no points to B).

Complete solution

   A v. B   B won on first innings
   A v. C   tie
   B v. C   C won

20 Addition

Letters for Digits, Two Numbers

$$\begin{array}{ccc} P & M & A \\ P & M & A \\ \hline R & P & M \end{array}$$

Since R, P and M are all even, there cannot be 1 to carry.
Suppose A = 2, then M = 4.
And P = M+M = 8.
∴ R = P+P = 16.
But the number below P+P is less than 10.
∴ A must be less than 2,
∴ A = 1.
∴ M = 2, ∴ P = 4, ∴ R = 8.

Complete solution

$$\begin{array}{ccc} 4 & 2 & 1 \\ 4 & 2 & 1 \\ \hline 8 & 4 & 2 \end{array}$$

21 C is Silent

Suppose B's statement true ('A is a Pukka'). Then A's statement would be true and C would be a Pukka. But this is not possible for all three would then make true statements.
∴ B's statement is false, and A is not a Pukka.
∴ neither A nor B is a Pukka, ∴ C is a Pukka.

∴ A's statement is true, ∴ A must be a Shilli-Shalla.
∴ B is a Wotta-Woppa.

Complete solution
  A is a Shilli-Shalla;
  B is a Wotta-Woppa;
  C is a Pukka.

22 Football

Three Teams, Old Method

A won both their matches, ∴ they cannot have drawn any.
∴ C's drawn match was against B.
  Suppose the score in that match was 0–0, then the score in
C v. A would have been 1–4. But A only scored 4 goals, and
they must have scored at least 1 against B, in order to beat
them. ∴ C v. B cannot have been 0–0, ∴ it must have been
1–1 (the only other possibility).
∴ C v. A was 0–3.
∴ A v. B must have been 1–0.

Complete solution
  A v. B   1–0
  A v. C   3–0
  B v. C   1–1

'B was twice as many places above A, as D was below C.'

Suppose D was one place below C, and that B was therefore two places above A. Then we have:

1	B	or	1	C	(if B were second and A
2			2	D	fourth, D and C cannot be
3	A		3	B	one place apart)
4	C		4		
5	D		5	A	

And E would be second or fourth – but neither of these is odd. ∴ D must be two places below C, and B must be four places above A. And we have:

1	B
2	C
3	
4	D
5	A

∴ E must be third.

Complete solution
1 Bert
2 Charlie
3 Ernie
4 Duggie
5 Alf

24 Division

Some Missing Figures

```
              – 1        (a)
    4 – ) – – – 9        (b)
              – –        (c)
         ─────────
              – –        (d)
              – –        (e)
         ─────────

              ───
```

Since the sum comes out exactly, the second figures of (*d*) and (*e*) are both 9.

And since (*e*) is the divisor multiplied by 1, the divisor must be 49. ∴ the first figure in (*a*) must be 2 and (*c*) must be 98. (The first figure in (*a*) cannot be more than 2, for (*c*) would then have three figures.)

Add up from the bottom and we get:

Complete solution

```
              2 1
    4 9 ) 1 0 2 9
            9 8
         ─────────
            4 9
            4 9
         ─────────

            ───
```

25 Addition

Letters for Digits, Two Numbers

(a)	(b)	(c)	(d)	(e)
	Q	X	X	Y
	A	P	X	X
P	M	Y	P	Q

The first digit of the answer must be 1 (the most that can be carried when 2 digits are added). $\therefore$ P = 1.

Consider (d). X must be 0 or 5. But it cannot be 0. (See (e); Y and Q would then be the same.) $\therefore$ X = 5.

$\therefore$ in (c), Y = 5+1+1 (carried) = 7.

$\therefore$ in (e), Q = 2.

And in (b), A = 8, M = 0.

Complete solution

```
  2 5 5 7
  8 1 5 5
 ─────────
1 0 7 1 2
```

26 Football

Four Teams, Old Method

C played one match, which they won 4–3. It could not have been against A, who only had 3 goals against, and it could not have been against D who only had 2 goals against.

$\therefore$ it was against B, and C v. B was 4–3.

∴ A did not play B or C, but only D; and similarly D only played A. And the score in A v. D was 2–3.

Complete solution
  A v. D   2–3
  B v. C   3–4

27 A Cross Number

1 Across must be 16, 36 or 64. But not 64 (see 1 Down). And if 16, then 1 Down would be 135, and 5 Across could only be 540. But there are no 0's.
∴ 1 Across must be 36, 1 Down is 357 and 5 Across is 714.
∴ 3 Across is 5–5.
And, from 4 Down, 2 Down must be 621.

Complete solution

1 3	2 6	//////
3 5	2	4 5
5 7	1	4

28 One of Each, and They All Speak ★

Consider B's statement. This cannot be true for A would then speak the truth, and A says he is a Shilli-Shalla. ∴ B's statement is false. ∴ A is not a Pukka.

∴ C is a Pukka (no one else can be).

∴ C's statement is true: B is a Wotta-Woppa, and A is a Shilli-Shalla.

Complete solution
    A is a Shilli-Shalla;
    B is a Wotta-Woppa;
    C is a Pukka.

29 Cricket ★

Three Teams

A's points can either be (10+2) or (6+6).

Suppose A's points were 6+6. Then A v. B was a win on first innings for A, ∴ B got 2 points. ∴ B (who got 10 points) got 8 points for their other match.

But there is no way of getting 8 points for a match.

∴ A's points must have been (10+2).

∴ Either B or C must have got 6 points against A. But not C, who only got 4 points.

∴ B beat A on first innings.

∴ A v. C was a win for A.

∴ B v. C was a tie on first innings (they both got 4 points).

Complete solution

   A v. B   B won on first innings
   A v. C   A won
   B v. C   tie on first innings

30 Addition

Letters for Digits, Two Numbers

$$
\begin{array}{ccc}
(a) & (b) & (c) \\
\mathrm{M} & \mathrm{B} & \mathrm{M} \\
\mathrm{B} & \mathrm{B} & \mathrm{M} \\
\hline
\mathrm{E} & \mathrm{X} & \mathrm{X}
\end{array}
$$

Consider (c). (M+M) is even, ∴ X is even. And since (B+B) is also even, there cannot be 1 to carry from (c) to (b).

M and B could be 1 and 6 (1+1 = 2; 6+6 = 12); or 2 and 7 (2+2 = 4; 7+7 = 14); or 3 and 8 (3+3 = 6; 8+8 = 16), and so on.

But if M and B were 2 and 7, then in (a) we would have E = 2+7+1 (that has been carried). But this makes E = 10, which is not possible.

∴ M can only be 1, and B = 6.
And X = 2, and E = 1+6+1 = 8.

Complete solution

  1 6 1
  6 6 1
  ―――
  8 2 2

31 Football

Three Teams, Old Method

C drew one, and had 4 goals for and 4 against, ∴ they cannot have played another match, for if they had they would have won it or lost it, and goals for would not be the same as goals against.

∴ C only played once and the score was 4–4.

∴ C's match was not against A, who only scored 4 goals, at least one of which must have been in the match which they won.

∴ C v. B was 4–4.

∴ B scored 2 goals against A (6 altogether).

And A scored 4 goals in their only match against B.

∴ A v. B was 4–2.

Complete solution
  A v. B 4–2
  B v. C 4–4

32 Division

Letters for Digits

```
            z e p      (a)              - - -
   p d ) y x q x z      (b)       - - ) - - - - -
           d b         (c)              - -
          -----                        -----
          p y x        (d)              - - -
          z h s        (e)              - - -
          -------                      -----
            y b z      (f)              - - -
            y y y      (g)              - - -
          -------                      -----
              p y      (h)                - -
          -------                        -----
```

(The reader is advised to draw a figure like the one on the right above, and to fill in the digits there as they are discovered.)

From (b) y = 1; ∴ from (f), (g) and (h) z = 2; ∴ from (d) and (e) p = 3. ∴ from (f), (g) and (h) b = 4. From (g) divisor is $\frac{111}{3} = 37$; ∴ d = 7. From (b), (c) and (d) q = 5, and x = 0. ∴ from (d), (e) and (f) s = 6, and h = 9; ∴ in (a) e = 8.

Complete solution

```
            2 8 3
   3 7 ) 1 0 5 0 2
          7 4
          -----
          3 1 0
          2 9 6
          -------
            1 4 2
            1 1 1
            -------
              3 1
            -------
```

33 A Cross Number

The digits of 4 Across are all even, and each one is less than the one before. ∴ 4 Across must start with 6 or 8. But not 8, for 1 Down is a square, and no square ends in 8.
∴ 4 Across must be 642.
∴ 2 Down must start with 3 (see also 1 Across).
And 1 Across is 13–.
   The first and last digits of 3 Down must add up to 17. And since all digits of 1 Across are odd, ∴ 3 Down is 928.
∴ 5 Across is 78.

Complete solution

	1		2		3	
1	1	2	3	3	9	
4	6		4		2	
▨		5	7		8	

34 Addition ★

Letters for Digits, Three Numbers

	(a)	(b)	(c)	(d)
		Y	M	B
		Y	M	B
		Y	M	B
	B	B	B	Y

The most that can be carried when three digits are added together is 2. ∴ B = 1 or 2.

Suppose B = 2. Then Y = B+B+B = 6.

∴ (b) = 6+6+6+(perhaps) 1 or 2 carried from (c).

The most that the first two figures of the answer could then be is 20. But according to our assumption (that B = 2) they should be 22.

∴ our assumption is wrong, ∴ B = 1, ∴ Y = 3. And (b) must be 3+3+3+2 = 11.

∴ in (c) M = 7.

Complete solution

```
    3 7 1
    3 7 1
    3 7 1
  ───────
  1 1 1 3
```

35 A was Absent ★

Suppose C's statement is true. Then B is a Pukka. And since what B says is therefore true, 'A is more truthful than C.'

∴ we have B (Pukka), A (Shilli-Shalla), and C (Wotta-Woppa).

∴ C's statement cannot be true ('B is a Pukka').

∴ Our assumption is incorrect and C's statement must be false.

∴ B is not a Pukka, and since C has made a false statement he is not a Pukka. ∴ A must be a Pukka.

∴ B's statement that A is more truthful than C is true.

∴ B must be a Shilli-Shalla and C must be a Wotta-Woppa.

Complete solution
  A   is a Pukka;
  B   is a Shilli-Shalla;
  C   is a Wotta-Woppa.

36 Football

Three Teams, Old Method

B won one but had as many goals against as for. ∴ B could
not have won or drawn their other match, but must have lost
it.

Since C had no goals against, C beat B. ∴ A's drawn match
was played against C. And we have:

	A	B	C
A	✕	l.	dr.
B	w.	✕	l.
C	dr.	w.	✕

C v. A was 0–0 (C had no goals scored against them).
∴ C v. B was 3–0 (see C's total of goals).
∴ B v. A was 4–1 (see B's total of goals).

Complete solution
  A v. B   1–4
  A v. C   0–0
  B v. C   0–3

Some Missing Figures

```
                - 3      (a)
   - -)- - 8 -           (b)
        - - -            (c)
        ───────
          8 -            (d)
          - -            (e)
          ─────
```

(*d*) and (*e*) are the divisor multiplied by 3.

∴ the divisor must be 27, 28 or 29 ($27 \times 3 = 81$, $29 \times 3 = 87$).

The last figure of (*c*) is 0, ∴ divisor must be 28.

(An odd number multiplied by a single figure cannot end in 0. But $28 \times 5 = 140$.)

And (*d*) and (*e*) are $3 \times 28 = 84$.

Add up from the bottom and we get:

Complete solution

```
            5 3
  2 8 ) 1 4 8 4
        1 4 0
        ───────
            8 4
            8 4
            ─────
```

38 Stealing, Breaking and Stopping

Denote window breaking by p; clock stopping by q; and pencil stealing by r.

Then we have: A, C, D → p, q   (a)
               A, B, C → r, p   (b)
               A, D   → q   (c)

In order to find who was responsible for r it will be best to find out who was there when there was no r, for we know that if the pencil stealer is there he will steal pencils. When there is no r, those present are A, C, and D.

∴ B is responsible for r.

Similarly from (c) p is not caused by A, D, but by B or C. But C is present in (a) and (b) (when p appears) and B is not.

∴ C is responsible for p.

Similarly from (b) q is not caused by A, B, C.

∴ D is responsible for q.

Complete solution
  Bert was the pencil stealer;
  Charlie was the window breaker;
  Duggie was the clock stopper.

39 Only One Out

	(a)	(b)	(c)	(d)	(e)	(f)
	2	1	6	6	4	8
		9	0	1	3	5
	1	3	7	8	0	

Consider (*f*). 0 must be 1, ∴ 8 must be 7 and 5 must be 6 to make the difference 1. ∴ we have:

$$
\begin{array}{r}
7 \\
6 \\
\hline
1 \\
\hline
\end{array}
$$

Consider (*e*). This must be:

$$
\begin{array}{r}
3 \\
4 \\
\hline
9 \\
\hline
\end{array}
$$

(If the figure on the first line is 5, and on the second line 2, the difference would only be 3, but it must be at least 7.)

Consider (*d*). Remember that 1 has been borrowed, so that difference is now 4. We must make them farther apart, thus:

$$
\begin{array}{r}
7 \\
0 \\
\hline
6 \\
\hline
\end{array}
$$

Consider (*c*). 0 can only be 1, ∴ we must have:

$$
\begin{array}{r}
5 \\
1 \\
\hline
4 \\
\hline
\end{array}
$$

Consider (*b*). 1 in the answer can only be 2 (it would not make sense to have 0 at the beginning of the answer). And 9 cannot go up, so it must be 8. ∴ we have:

$$
\begin{array}{r}
0 \\
8 \\
\hline
2 \\
\hline
\end{array}
$$

And (*a*) must be 1.

Complete solution
```
1 0 5 7 3 7
  8 1 0 4 6
───────────
  2 4 6 9 1
```

40 Addition   ★

Letters for Digits, Three Numbers

```
    (a) (b) (c)
     R   A   X
     A   A   X
     X   A   X
    ───────────
     M   P   M
```

Consider (*a*). Since there are no 1's, and R, A and X are all different, they must be at least 2, 3 and 4. But $2+3+4 = 9$.
∴ M must be 9, and R, A and X must be 2, 3 and 4, though we do not yet know which is which.

Since M = 9, from (*c*) X must be 3.

Consider (*b*). A cannot be 4, for $4+4+4 = 12$ and there would be 1 to carry. But we know there is not.
∴ A = 2; ∴ R = 4; and P = 6.

Complete solution
```
    4 2 3
    2 2 3
    3 2 3
   ───────
    9 6 9
```

41 Football

Three Teams, New Method

A cannot have got more than 5 points for wins or draws.
C cannot have got more than 5 points for wins or draws.
B cannot have got more than 20 points for wins and draws
for they can only have played two matches.
∴ A got 5 points for wins or draws, and 4 points for goals.
   B got 20 points for wins or draws and 6 points for goals.
   C got 5 points for wins or draws and 2 points for goals.
B must have won against A and against C, and C v. A must
have been a draw.
∴ C v. A was 1–1, and C v. B was 1–?.
A got 4 goals, ∴ A v. B was 3–?.
B got 6 goals, ∴ B v. C was 2–1, and B v. A was 4–3.
(The only possibilities since B won both matches.)

Complete solution
   A v. B   3–4
   A v. C   1–1
   B v. C   2–1

42 A Cross Number

Consider 3 Down. This is 5 times some number, ∴ it must end in 0 or 5.

But there are no 0's, ∴ it must be 5.

From 1 Across the first figure of 1 Down is even. It cannot be 4 or more (see 5 Across) ∴ it must be 2.

1 Down must be 25 and 5 Across 75.

3 Down is 5 times 5 Across, ∴ it is 375.

4 Across must be 567; and 2 Down is 767.

Complete solution

1	2	3
2	7	3
4		
5	6	7
////	5	
	7	5

43 Not Talking Much

Suppose C's statement is true. Then A is a Pukka, so that his statement is true, and B is a Shilli-Shalla, ∴ all three of them make true statements. But this is not possible, for one of them is a Wotta-Woppa.

∴ C's statement is false: A is not a Pukka. ∴ B must be a Pukka (no one else can be). ∴ C is not a Wotta-Woppa, ∴ C is a Shilli-Shalla and A is a Wotta-Woppa.

Complete solution

A is a Wotta-Woppa;

B is a Pukka;

C is a Shilli-Shalla.

44 Division

Letters for Digits

```
          x c d y      (a)              - - - -
    n m)n n r m b a    (b)         - -)- - - - - -
      n b r            (c)              - - -
      ───────                          ─────
        n b m          (d)              - - -
        d n            (e)              - -
      ───────                          ─────
          n y b        (f)              - - -
          n n c        (g)              - - -
        ─────                          ─────
            m a        (h)              - -
            y p        (i)              - -
          ─────                        ─────
              d        (j)                -
          ─────                        ─────
```

(The reader is advised to draw a figure like the one on the right above, and to fill in the digits there as they are discovered.)

From (d) n = 1; from (b), (c) and (d) b = 0. From (f) and (g) since n = 1, y = 2; ∴ from (h) and (i) m = 3; ∴ in (g) c = 7. And since divisor is 13, (e), 7 times the divisor, is 91, and d = 9. (i) must be 26, ∴ p = 6; and in (h) a = 5. 8×13 = 104, ∴ in (a) x = 8, and in (c) r = 4.

Complete solution

```
            8 7 9 2
1 3 ) 1 1 4 3 0 5
      1 0 4
      ─────
        1 0 3
          9 1
        ─────
          1 2 0
          1 1 7
          ─────
              3 5
              2 6
              ─────
                9
```

45 Addition ★

Letters for Digits, Two Numbers

```
Q Q Z
L Q Z
─────
E L L
```

Consider the last digit in the answer. L must be even, ∴ it must be at least 2. If L = 2, then Z = 1, and Q = 6 (6+6 = 12). (Not the other way round, for if Z were 6 there would be 1 to carry, and the second digit of the answer would not be the same as the third.) And if Q = 6 and L = 2, then E would be 9 (6+2+1 (carried)). But if L were more than 2, for example 4, the first (hundreds) column would be (7+4+1), which would mean that there would be four figures in the answer.

∴ L = 2, Z = 1, Q = 6 and E = 9.

    6 6 1
    2 6 1
    ───────
    9 2 2

46 Football

Four Teams, Old Method

D played everyone, but A and B only played D, ∴ C can only have played D (there is no one else for them to play).
∴ C v. D was 2–2.

Since B got 2 points, B beat D, and since D got 3 points, D beat A.

Since A only had 1 goal scored against them, D v. A was 1–0.

D got 4 goals, 2 against C, 1 against A, so they must have scored 1 against B. And since B got 3 goals, B v. D was 3–1.

Complete solution
    A v. D   0–1
    B v. D   3–1
    C v. D   2–2

47 Who Does What in Our Factory

With a diagram this becomes a very simple problem. Thus:

	D-Op	D-Sh	D-K-P	B-W	W O	S-U	Worker
A				X			X
B	X		X	X			X
C							
D	X	X		X	X		
E							
F	X		X				X
G							

Information about A, F, B and D has been inserted in diagram. The reader is advised to insert information about D-Sh, S-U, etc., in his own diagram.

It will then be seen that E must be the Worker; ∴ no one else can be. Fill in this information and it will be seen that A is D-K-P. And then, in succession, C is D-O; F is D-Sh; G is B-W; B is W O; D is S-U.

Complete solution

    Alf is the Door-Knob-Polisher;
    Bert is the Welfare Officer;
    Charlie is the Door-Opener;
    Duggie is the Sweeper-Upper;
    Ernie is the Worker;
    Fred is the Door-Shutter;
    George is the Bottle-Washer.

48 Pocket-Money on the ★ Island of Imperfection

Since B(1) is true, A is a Shilli-Shalla.

∴ A and B both make true statements.

∴ C is a Wotta-Woppa, A is a Shilli-Shalla and B is a Pukka.

    From C(2) (false), A's second statement is true, ∴ A's first statement is false.

    From A(1) and C(1) (both false), A's and B's pocket-money must be equal.

    And from A(2) (true), B's pocket-money is 50 Hopes,

∴ A's pocket-money is 50 Hopes.

    ∴ from B(2) (true), C's pocket-money is 25 Hopes.

Complete solution

    A is a Shilli-Shalla; his pocket-money is 50 Hopes.
    B is a Pukka; his pocket-money is 50 Hopes.
    C is a Wotta-Woppa; his pocket-money is 25 Hopes.

49 Uncle Bungle Shows that He Can Get Division Sums Wrong Too!

```
              2 9      (a)
      8 4 ) 2 2 2 3    (b)
            6 2        (c)
          ─────
            6 9 3      (d)
            4 9 3      (e)
          ─────
```

Remember that all figures are 1 out. The first figure of (*a*) must be 1 or 3; and the first figure in the divisor must be 7 or 9. ∴ (*c*) cannot be the divisor multiplied by 3 (it would have to have three figures). ∴ the first digit in (*a*) is 1. And the divisor is 7−.

The second figure in the divisor is 1 more or less than 2, and 1 more or less than 4. ∴ the divisor is 73.

The second figure in (*a*) can only be 8, ∴ (*d*) and (*e*) are 73 × 8, i.e. 584.

Add up from the bottom and we get:

Complete solution

```
            1 8
    7 3 ) 1 3 1 4
          7 3
        ─────
          5 8 4
          5 8 4
        ─────
```

50 Addition

Letters for Digits, Two Numbers

$$
\begin{array}{ccccc}
(a) & (b) & (c) & (d) & (e) \\
 & R & P & A & P \\
 & A & B & B & M \\
\hline
R & R & R & R & P \\
\end{array}
$$

The most that can be carried when adding two digits is 1, ∴ the first R in the answer is 1, ∴ all the other R's are 1.

Consider (e). P+M = P, ∴ M = 0 (but we cannot yet say what P is). Note that there is nothing to carry.

From (b) R+A+(perhaps) 1 = 11. ∴ A must be 9, and there is 1 carried from (c).

We know that A+B = 11. ∴ B = 2.

And P+B+1 = 11, ∴ P = 8.

Complete solution

$$
\begin{array}{r}
1\ 8\ 9\ 8 \\
9\ 2\ 2\ 0 \\
\hline
1\ 1\ 1\ 1\ 8 \\
\end{array}
$$

51 A Cross Number

The second digit of 1 Across is at least 2; ∴ the second digit of 2 Down is at least 4 (see 2 Down and 3 Across). ∴ the third digit of 2 Down is at least 5.

3 Down must be 27 or 64. But the first figure of 4 Across cannot be 7 for 4 Across would then be 7–5, but the sum of the digits is 11.

∴ 3 Down is 64.

Since 1 Down is even, 4 Across must be 425, 2 Down must be 245, and 1 Across must be 72.

And from 1 Down and 3 Across, 1 Down must be 782.

Complete solution

	1 7	2 2
3 6	8	4
4 4	2	5

52 Football ★

Three Teams, New Method

3 matches were played, ∴ 30 points were given for wins and draws.

C cannot have got more than 5 points for wins or draws, ∴ C scored 3 goals.

B cannot have got more than 10 points for wins or draws, ∴ B scored 5 goals.

And A cannot have got more than 15 points for wins or draws, ∴ A scored 7 goals.

Since B did not lose a match, both their matches were draws and A won the third match against C.

C only scored 3 goals, so we have:

	A	B	C
A	✕	dr.	w. ?-1 ?-2
B	dr.	✕	dr. 2-2 1-1
C	l. 1-? 2-?	dr. 2-2 1-1	✕

If B v. C was 1–1, then B v. A would be 4–4, – but not more than 7 goals were scored in any match.

∴ B v. C was 2–2, and B v. A was 3–3.

∴ A scored 4 goals against C (7 altogether), ∴ A v. C was 4–1.

Complete solution
  A v. B   3–3
  A v. C   4–1
  B v. C   2–2

53 The Good Worker

G says that F is the Worker. This cannot be true, for there would then be two people who have told the truth, G and the Worker (F). ∴ G's statement is false, and F is *not* the Worker.

∴ E is the Worker.
And since E's statement is true, G is the Door-Shutter.
∴ F must be the Door-Opener.

Complete solution
  Ernie is the Worker;
  Fred is the Door-Opener;
  George is the Door-Shutter.

54 Still Only One Out

$$
\begin{array}{cccc}
(a) & (b) & (c) & (d) \\
2 & 9 & 1 & 0 \\
1 & 4 & 9 & 7 \\
\hline
2 & 1 & 0 & 6 \\
\end{array}
$$

Consider (d). 0 must be 1; ∴ the other two figures must add up to 11. ∴ 7 must be 6 and 6 must be 5.

  Consider (c). 0 must be 1. And 9 must be 8. ∴ 1 must be 0 (remember that there was 1 to borrow).

  Consider (b). 9 must be 8. And remembering that there was 1 to borrow, 4 must be 5 and 1 must be 2.

  Consider (a). 1 must be 2 (we cannot have 0 at the beginning of the line). ∴ the first 2 must be 3 (it must be more than 2). ∴ the second 2 is 1.

Complete solution

$$
\begin{array}{cccc}
3 & 8 & 0 & 1 \\
2 & 5 & 8 & 6 \\
\hline
1 & 2 & 1 & 5 \\
\end{array}
$$

55 Addition

Letters for Digits, Two Numbers

```
          (a) (b) (c) (d) (e)
               D  T  S  U
               D  N  N  U
             ─────────────
             U  T  D  N  T
```

The most that can be carried when two digits are added together is 1. ∴ U = 1. ∴ from (e) T = U+U = 2.

∴ D+D = 12, and D = 6 (there could not have been 1 to carry, for D+D must be even).

From (d) S = 0, and there is nothing to carry to (c).

∴ N = 4.

Complete solution

```
     6  2  0  1
     6  4  4  1
  ─────────────
  1  2  6  4  2
```

Division

Some Missing Figures

```
            3 - -      (a)
    - -)- - 0 - 0      (b)
        - -            (c)
        ____
         - -           (d)
         - -           (e)
        ____
        - - -          (f)
        - - -          (g)
        ____
```

(*c*) must be 9–, and since this is 3 times the divisor, the divisor is 3–.

The second figure of divisor cannot be 0, for there would then be three figures in (*d*); nor can it be 5 for 95 is not a multiple of 3. ∴ Since divisor goes exactly into (*f*), which ends in 0, it must be even, ∴ it must be 32 (since 34 times 3 is more than 100). ∴ (*c*) is 96. ∴ (*f*) and (*g*) are 32×5 = 160.

And since the first figure of (*d*) is 4, (*e*) is 32.

Add up from the bottom and we get:

Complete solution

```
            3 1 5
    3 2)1 0 0 8 0
        9 6
        ____
          4 8
          3 2
        ____
        1 6 0
        1 6 0
        ____
```

232

57 Football

Three Teams, Old Method

Since B got 4 points, both matches were won. And since they scored only 2 goals more than the goals scored against them, each match was won by 1 goal.

    Consider A v. C. A won none, ∴ A did not win; but C got no points. ∴ this match cannot have been drawn or won by C. ∴ A v. C has not been played.

    C had 2 goals scored against them in C v. B (C's only match).

    And since each match was won by 1 goal, C v. B was 1–2.

    And, from B's goals, B v. A was 3–2.

Complete solution
    A v. B   2–3
    B v. C   2–1

58 The Breathless B

A says he is a Wotta-Woppa. But this cannot be true for Wotta-Woppas do not tell the truth. Therefore he is not a Wotta-Woppa. He cannot be a Pukka for in that case his statement would be true.

∴ A must be a Shilli-Shalla.

∴ C's statement that A is a Shilli-Shalla is true.

∴ C is a Pukka.

∴ B must be a Wotta-Woppa.

Complete solution

    A is a Shilli-Shalla;

    B is a Wotta-Woppa;

    C is a Pukka.

59 Letters for Digits   ★

A Multiplication

$$
\begin{array}{r}
\text{Z Y Y P M} \\
\text{M} \\
\hline
\text{A A Z E Y M}
\end{array}
$$

The only digits which when multiplied by themselves produce a number ending in the same digits are 1, 5 and 6. ∴ M must be one of these. But Y is half of M, ∴ M must be even, ∴ M = 6, ∴ Y = 3.

    $6 \times 6 = 36$, ∴ for the answer to end in 36, P must be 0 or 5. But we are told that P is less than 3. ∴ P = 0.

    $6 \times 3 = 18$, ∴ E = 8.

    ∴ Z = 8 + 1 = 9.

    $6 \times 9 = 54$, and there is 1 to carry. ∴ AA = 55.

Complete solution

$$
\begin{array}{r}
9\ 3\ 3\ 0\ 6 \\
6 \\
\hline
5\ 5\ 9\ 8\ 3\ 6
\end{array}
$$

60 Addition

Letters for Digits, Two Numbers

```
        (a) (b) (c) (d) (e)
             M   B   B
         S   K   K   B
        ─────────────────
     M   W   W   X   K
```

When two numbers are added together the most that can be carried is 1.

∴ M = 1.

   Since the most that can be carried is 1, S = 9, and W = 0.

   Since K, in (*d*), is not 9, it must be 8.

   Consider (*e*): B+B = 8 or 18. It cannot be 18, for B would then be 9, and S = 9. ∴ B = 4.

∴ X must be 2.

Complete solution

```
        1 4 4
      9 8 8 4
    ───────────
    1 0 0 2 8
```

Letters for Digits

```
                r x g d      (a)
     x g ) t h s f g g       (b)
           t r r             (c)
           ─────
             t x f           (d)
             t f j           (e)
             ─────
               d d g         (f)
               d t g         (g)
               ─────
                 t f g       (h)
                 s d         (i)
                 ─────
                   x r       (j)
```

(The reader is advised to draw a figure like the one on the
right above, where the digits can be inserted as they are
found.)

From (*f*), (*g*) and (*h*) f = 0. From (*h*) t = 1. From (*f*), (*g*)
and (*h*) t+t = d, ∴ d = 2. From (*d*), (*e*) and (*f*) x = 3. From
(*h*), (*i*) and (*j*) s = 7 (since we know that g cannot be 0, 1 or 2).
From (*b*), (*c*) and (*d*) r = 4. From (*h*), (*i*) and (*j*) g = 6. From
(*e*) j = 8. From (*b*), (*c*) and (*d*) h = 5.

```
          4 3 6 2
36) 1 5 7 0 6 6
      1 4 4
        1 3 0
        1 0 8
          2 2 6
          2 1 6
            1 0 6
              7 2
              3 4
```

62 Football ★

Four Teams, New Method

Neither B nor C can have got any points for wins or draws. A can only have got 15 (out of their 20), and D can only have got 25 (out of their 30).

But $15 + 25 = 40$, and this is the number of points for wins or draws for four games.

D with 25 points for wins or draws must have won 2 and drawn 1, ∴ they played everybody, including C.

But C, with 1 point, only played one match, ∴ C v. A and C v. B were the matches that have not been played.

D's drawn match must have been against A (B and C won none and drew none), and D beat B and C.

Since D only scored 5 goals, D v. B was 2–1, D v. C was 2–1, and D v. A was 1–1.

A only scored 1 goal against D, ∴ A scored 4 goals against B.

B only scored 1 goal against D, ∴ B scored 3 goals against A. ∴ A v. B was 4–3.

Complete solution
  A v. B   4–3
  A v. D   1–1
  B v. D   1–2
  C v. D   1–2

63 Who was X?

E was as many places before C as G was before A, ∴ C and A were not first and E and G were not fourth.
Also E was not first and A was not second.
∴ since A, C and E were not first, G was first.
∴ A cannot be fourth (G would then be three places before A and E would only be one place before C).
∴ C was fourth (no one else can be).
∴ E was second (two places before C)
and A was third (two places after G).

Complete solution
  1 George
  2 Ernie
  3 Alf
  4 Charlie
    Charlie was X.

Consider 5 Across and 2 Down. 5 Across must be an even multiple of 19, i.e. 38 or 76. But it cannot be 76 (see 1 Down, and remember there are no 0's).

∴ 5 Across is 38.

∴ 1 Across is $38 \times 7 = 266$ and 1 Down is 233.

3 Down (a multiple of 13) can only be 65.

∴ 4 Across must be 345.

Complete solution

1 2	2 6	3 6
4 3	4	5
5 3	8	////

65 Cricket

Three Teams

Each team played two matches.

A can only have got 11 points by drawing one (5) and winning one on first innings (6).

The only way in which C can have got 7 points is by drawing one (5) and losing one on first innings (2).

Suppose that A v. C was a draw. Then A's other match was against B and since A got 6 points, B got 2. C's other match was against B, and since C got 2 points, B got 6. But B's points are 10, not 2+6. ∴ A v. C was not a draw, ∴ A's drawn match was against B, and C's drawn match was against B (making B's points 10).

And A v. C was a win on first innings for A.

Complete solution
  A v. B   tie
  A v. C   A won on first innings
  B v. C   tie

66 Division ★

Some Missing Figures

```
         – 5 –       (a)
– –)6 – – –          (b)
       – –           (c)
      ‾‾‾‾
     – – –           (d)
      – –            (e)
     ‾‾‾‾‾
     – 7 –           (f)
    – – –            (g)
   ‾‾‾‾‾
```

(e) is the divisor times 5. But since (e) only has two figures the divisor must be less than 20. From (f) –7– is a multiple of the divisor but 18×9 is only 162, ∴ the divisor must be 19, and (f) and (g) are 171.

Since (d) has three figures and (e) has two, (e) must be the two-figure multiple of 19 nearest to 100, i.e. 95 (19×5). (d) starts with 1, ∴ the first figure of (c) must be 4 or 5. But it cannot be 4, for there is no two-figure multiple of 19 starting with 4. ∴ (c) is 57 (19×3).

Add up from the bottom and we get:

Complete solution

```
        3 5 9
1 9 ) 6 8 2 1
      5 7
      ─────
      1 1 2
        9 5
      ─────
        1 7 1
        1 7 1
      ─────
```

67 Addition

Letters for Digits, Two Numbers

```
        (a) (b) (c)
         Z   B   B
         B   Y   B
        ───────────
         C   Z   Z
```

Consider (b) *and* (c). If B were less than 5, then there would be nothing to carry from (c) to (b) and Y would be equal to B. But this is not possible. ∴ B is greater than 5.

Suppose B = 6, then Z = 2, and (a) is 2+6, so that C is 8 or 9.

If B were 7, then Z would be 4 and Z+B would be greater than 9.

∴ B = 6, Z = 2, Y = 5, C = 9.

Complete solution

```
 2 6 6
 6 5 6
 ─────
 9 2 2
```

68 Football

Four Teams, Consecutive Saturdays

Consider the second Saturday. Only 2 goals were scored against C altogether, ∴ C must have played D (and had 1 goal scored against them).

∴ on the second Saturday, C played D (0–1); and A played B (4–3).

On the first Saturday, C cannot have had more than 1 goal scored against them.

∴ C played A (2–1); and B played D (3–2).

And on the third Saturday, A played D (4–1); and B played C (0–4).

Complete solution

A v. B   4–3
A v. C   1–2
A v. D   4–1
B v. C   0–4
B v. D   3–2
C v. D   0–1

69 The Running-Backward
Race

Suppose E was second. Then D would have to be first. But if B was third, A and C would have to be fourth and fifth, so that the difference between D and B would not be the same as the difference between A and C.

It can similarly be seen that it is not possible for E to be fourth and, as E was not first or third, E can only be fifth.

B was not second, ∴ D must have been first, A second, B third and C fourth.

Complete solution

1 Duggie
2 Alf
3 Bert
4 Charlie
5 Ernie

70 More Pocket-Money on the ★ Island of Imperfection

We are told that B(1) is false, ∴ A is not a Shilli-Shalla. C(1) cannot be true, for if it were then C is a Wotta-Woppa and all his statements are false.

Since B and C both make false statements, A must be a Pukka, and from C(1) (false), C is not a Wotta-Woppa, ∴ B is a Wotta-Woppa and C is a Shilli-Shalla.

A(1) is true, ∴ B's pocket-money is twice C's.

C(2) is true, ∴ C's pocket-money is three-quarters of A's.

∴ C's pocket-money is less than A's.

∴ from A(2), C's pocket-money is 30 Hopes.

∴ from A(1), B's pocket-money is 60 Hopes.

and from C(2), A's pocket-money is 40 Hopes.

Complete solution

A is a Pukka; his pocket-money is 40 Hopes.

B is a Wotta-Woppa; his pocket-money is 60 Hopes.

C is a Shilli-Shalla; his pocket-money is 30 Hopes.

71 Football

Four Teams, Old Method

Consider D. They lost none and drew none; but their goals for were only 1 more than their goals against, ∴ they can only have played one match, which must have been against C (who played everyone) and the score was 2–1.

Consider A. They won none and drew one, and had the same number of goals for as against.

∴ they cannot have lost any, for, if they had, their goals against would have been more than their goals for.

∴ they only played one, which must have been against C, and the score was 3–3.

∴ B can only have played one match, against C (there is no one else for them to play).

And C v. B was 3–0 ((7−3−1)−(5−3−2))

Complete solution

    A v. C   3–3
    B v. C   0–3
    C v. D   1–2

72 Addition

Letters for Digits, Two Numbers

$$
\begin{array}{cccc}
  & R & A & A & P \\
  & G & G & A & P \\
\hline
P & M & B & M & R \\
\end{array}
$$

The most that can be carried when two digits are added together is 1. $\therefore$ P = 1.

$\therefore$ R = P+P = 2.

Suppose G = 9, then 9+2 (plus, perhaps, 1 which has been carried) cannot be more than 12. But M cannot be 1 or 2, for P = 1, and R = 2.

$\therefore$ M must be 0.

$\therefore$ A+A = 10, and A = 5.

$\therefore$ there is 1 to carry from A+G (for G is at least 7).

$\therefore$ G = 7 (2+7+1 = 10) and B = 3.

Complete solution

```
   2 5 5 1
   7 7 5 1
  ────────
1 0 3 0 2
```

73 All is Confusion – but the Bottle-Washer was Third

(i) The Bottle-Washer was third.

(ii) From (2) the Worker was fifth (no one else can be).

(iii) $\therefore$ from (1) the Door-Opener was fourth, and B was first.

(iv) From (3) C was fifth (not A from (1), not (D) from (4) since the Door-Shutter was first or second, and not E from (5). $\therefore$ the Door-Knob-Polisher was second.

(v) $\therefore$ the Door-Shutter was first (no one else can be). $\therefore$ from (4), D was second.

(vi) $\therefore$ from (5), E was fourth and A was third.

Complete solution

1. Bert (Door-Shutter)
2. Duggie (Door-Knob-Polisher)
3. Alf (Bottle-Washer)
4. Ernie (Door-Opener)
5. Charlie (Worker)

74 Multiply by 4

$$
\begin{array}{r}
\text{C B D F} \quad (a) \\
4 \\
\hline
\text{D F D E D} \quad (b)
\end{array}
$$

D, the last digit of (*b*), must be even, since (*a*) has been multiplied by 4. But D, the first digit of (*b*), cannot be more than 3 (9999×4 starts with 3), and since D is even, D = 2.

F could be 3 or 8 (4×3 = 12, 4×8 = 32). Suppose F = 8, then there is 3 to carry and E = 1 (8+3 = 11), and the third figure in (*b*), D, would be odd. But D = 2. ∴ F cannot be 8, ∴ F = 3. And E = (4×2)+1 = 9.

The first two figures of (*b*) are 23, ∴ C = 5, and there must have been 3 to carry. ∴ B = 8.

Complete solution

$$
\begin{array}{r}
5\ 8\ 2\ 3 \\
4 \\
\hline
2\ 3\ 2\ 9\ 2
\end{array}
$$

75 Cause and Effect ★★

We have: A, C, F → q, r   (a)
B, C, D, F → s, r   (b)
B, D, E → p, s   (c)
A, D, E, F → p, q   (d)

Consider p: from (a) and (b), p is *not* caused by A, B, C, D, F.
∴ p is caused by E.
  Consider q: from (b) and (c), q is *not* caused by B, C, D, E, F.
∴ q is caused by A.
  Consider r: from (c) and (d), r is *not* caused by A, B, D, E, F.
∴ r is caused by C.
  Consider s: from (a) and (d), s is *not* caused by A, C, D, E, F.
∴ s is caused by B.

Complete solution
  p is caused by E
  q is caused by A
  r is caused by C
  s is caused by B

76 Two, Four, Six, Eight ★★

```
              2 -     (a)
    4 -)- - - 8       (b)
        - - -         (c)
        _____
          - -         (d)
          6 -         (e)
```

Look first for figure that is wrong. $49 \times 2 = 98$; $\therefore$ either 4 or 2 is wrong. And either 4 or 6 is wrong, for $4- \times 1$ is $4-$, and $4- \times 2$ would be at least $8-$.

$\therefore$ as only one figure is wrong, it must be 4.

$\therefore$ as (*c*) (three figures) is divisor times 2, (*d*) and (*e*) must be the divisor.

$\therefore$ the divisor is 68, and the second figure in (*a*) is 1.

$\therefore$ (*c*) (divisor times 2) $= 136$.

Add up from the bottom and we get:

Complete solution

The figure 4 was wrong.

```
            2 1
    6 8 ) 1 4 2 8
          1 3 6
            6 8
            6 8
```

77 Football

Three Teams, Old Method

Since the total of goals against must be the same as the total of goals for, B have 5 goals scored against them.

A and B scored 7 goals $(5+2)$ and C had 4 goals scored against them.

$\therefore$ A and B must have scored 3 goals $(7-4)$ in their match against each other.

$\therefore$ A v. B could not have been a draw.

$\therefore$ B v. C was the drawn match.

And since B has 2 goals for and 5 goals against, B lost their other match (against A) by 3 goals. And since 'A and B must have scored 3 goals in their match against each other' (see

above), A v. B was 3–0; ∴ A v. C was 2–4 and B v. C was
2–2.

Complete solution

  A v. B   3–0
  A v. C   2–4
  B v. C   2–2

78 A Cross Number

3 Across and 4 Down are both perfect squares. And from 5
Across, 4 Down is even.

∴ 4 Down must be 16, 36 or 64. ∴ 3 Across must be 81, 36
or 16.

But not 81 (see 2 Down and 5 Across; last digit of 2 Down
must be at least 8).

And not 16 (see 2 Down).

∴ 3 Across is 36, and 4 Down is 64.

1 Across must be 12 (not 18, see 2 Down). The third digit of
2 Down must be 4, 6 or 8, but not 4 or 8 (see 5 Across),
∴ it is 6.

∴ 5 Across is 264.

And 1 Down is 192.

Complete solution

1 1	2 2	//////
9	3 3	4 6
5 2	6	4

Letters for Digits, Two Numbers

$$(a)\ (b)\ (c)\ (d)\ (e)$$
$$\text{E H R G}$$
$$\text{M H R G}$$
$$\overline{\text{M D M E E}}$$

The first figure in the answer must be 1, the most that can be carried when two digits are added together. ∴ M = 1.

In (b), since M = 1, E must be 8 or 9, and since D cannot be 1 it must be 0. ∴ D = 0.

From (e) E must be even. ∴ E = 8.

And since there cannot be anything to carry from (e) to (d), G = 4 and R = 9. And from (c) H = 5.

Complete solution
```
    8 5 9 4
    1 5 9 4
  ─────────
  1 0 1 8 8
```

80 A Competition

Since neither C nor E was third or fifth, we have:

```
        1
        2
        3   A, B, D
        4
        5   A, B, D
```

But A was above B, ∴ A was not fifth, and D is above E, ∴ D was not fifth.

∴ B was fifth.

∴ either A or D was third.

Suppose D was third; then E was fourth, so that D was one place above E. But it is not possible for A to be one place above B. ∴ D was not third.

∴ A was third.

And since A was two places above B, D was two places above E.

∴ D was second, E was fourth and C was first.

Complete solution
1 Charlie
2 Duggie
3 Alf
4 Ernie
5 Bert

81 Division

Figures All Wrong

```
        3 8      (a)
   2 3)8 7 5     (b)
        7 7      (c)
      ─────
        2 1 5    (d)
        4 1 5    (e)
      ─────
```

(*d*) and (*e*) must both be the same. And since the figures are only 1 out, (*d*) and (*e*) must both be 3--.

Divisor starts with 1 or 3. If 1, the most it can be is 14. And (*d*) and (*e*) cannot then be more than 14 × 9 = 126.

∴ the divisor cannot start with 1, but must start with 3. If the divisor were 32 then (*d*) and (*e*) could not be more than 32 × 9 = 288.

∴ the divisor must be 34, not 32. And the second figure in (*a*) must be 9 (for 34 × 7 is only 238).

∴ (*d*) and (*e*) are 306.

If the first figure in (*a*) were 4 then (*c*) would have three figures (34 × 4 = 136).

∴ the first figure in (*a*) is 2, and (*c*) is 68.

Add up from the bottom and we get:

Complete solution

```
          2 9
  3 4 ) 9 8 6
        6 8
        ─────
        3 0 6
        3 0 6
        ─────
```

82 Football

Three Teams, New Method

The points are: A – 8
B – 14
C – 9

The greatest number of points that they can get for wins or draws is: A – 5, B – 10, C – 5. ∴ only two matches were played (not one, for in that case one of them would have got *no* points).

Suppose that B drew two matches, against A and C, then

B's total of goals should equal (A+C)'s total. But B's total is 4, and A's is 3 and C's is 4.

∴ A v. C was a draw and B won one.

Either A or C played only one game, and since A got 3 goals and C got 4, A v. C must have been 3–3. And C scored 1 goal against B.

∴ B v. C was 4–1.

Complete solution
  A v. C   3–3
  B v. C   4–1

83 Serjeant Simple Loses his Wallet

Remember that from 'If p, then q' it does not follow that 'If q, then p.' (For example, from 'If that animal is a cow, then it has four legs' it does *not* follow that 'If that animal has four legs, then it is a cow.')

But from 'If p, then q', 'If *not* q, then *not* p' does follow. (Using the same example, 'If that animal has *not* got four legs, then it is *not* a cow'.)

(1) is equivalent to: 'If you find your wallet it is because you have not looked in the deep freeze.' That is, 'If you look in the deep freeze you will *not* find your wallet.'

(2) is equivalent to: 'If you look behind the desk you will find your wallet.'

(3) is in the form 'Not both p and q', from which we can deduce 'If p then *not* q.' ∴ it is equivalent to 'If you look in the cycle shed you will *not* find your wallet.'

Complete solution
Serjeant Simple's wallet is behind the desk.

84 Addition

Letters for Digits, Two Numbers

(a)	(b)	(c)	(d)	(e)	(f)
Z	Z	Y	B	R	R
Z	Z	Y	Z	R	R
Y	Y	X	X	Q	Z

Consider (f). Z must be even; ∴ Z = 2, 4, 6 or 8. (Z cannot be 0, for there cannot be a 0 in (a).) But not 6 or 8, for in that case there would be another figure before the first Y in the answer.

Whether Z is 2 or 4 there cannot be 1 to carry from (b).

Suppose Z = 4. Then Y would be 8, and there would be 1 to carry from (c). But there is not (if there were the answer would start with 89).

∴ Z is not 4, ∴ Z = 2, ∴ Y = 4.

If R were 1, there would not be 1 to carry from (f). But there is. ∴ R = 6, and Q = 3.

In (c) X must be 8 or 9. ∴ in (d) B must be 5 or 6. But not 6, for R = 6.

∴ B = 5, and X = 8.

Complete solution

```
  2 2 4 5 6 6
  2 2 4 2 6 6
  _____
  4 4 8 8 3 2
```

85 A Cross Number ★★

Consider 4 Down. Perfect squares of two figures starting with an odd number (see 3 Across) are 16 and 36. But from 3 Across 4 Down must be 36, and 3 Across must be 123.

The only factors of 3 Across (123) are 3 and 41.

∴ 1 Across must be 41.

5 Across is 41–(1 Down) multiplied by an even number, ∴ it must be 41 × 2, and since 5 Across ends in 6, 1 Down is 418 and 5 Across is 836.

Complete solution

1 4	2 1	
3 1	2	4 3
5 8	3	6

86 Division ★★

Some Missing Figures

```
         3 - - -        (a)
- -)- - - - 5 -         (b)
      - -                (c)
      -----
      - - -              (d)
      - -                (e)
      -----
        - -              (f)
        - -              (g)
```

The first figure of (*d*) must be 1, ∴ (*c*) is 99 and (*b*) starts 100. And since (*c*) is 3 times the divisor, the divisor is 33, and (*e*) must be 99. Since the last figure of (*d*) is 5, the first figure of (*f*) is 6, and (*f*) and (*g*) are 66.

Add up from the bottom and we get:

Complete solution

```
              3 0 3 2
    3 3 ) 1 0 0 0 5 6
          9 9
          ─────
              1 0 5
                9 9
              ─────
                  6 6
                  6 6
                  ─────
```

87 They All Compete

We are told that B is as many places above D as F is above A, and that D is above F. ∴ B, D and F are all above A. Also A's place is odd and A is above E.

∴ A is not seventh (he could not be above E).

∴ A must be fifth (not third, for B, D and F are all above him).

∴ F is fourth (not third, for B would then have to be two places above D, who must be above F).

Since D's place is even, D must be second and B first. C's place is even, but the only even place left is sixth.

∴ C is sixth. And since E is below A, E is seventh.

∴ G is third.

Complete solution

1 Bert
2 Duggie
3 George
4 Fred
5 Alf
6 Charlie
7 Ernie

88 Football

Four Teams, Old Method

B played two and drew one, and the goals were 3–0, ∴ their drawn match was 0–0, and B won their other match 3–0.

The number of matches drawn must be even, for each match appears twice. C cannot have drawn both matches (see their goals), ∴ they drew none. ∴ B v. A was a draw, and the score was 0–0.

B's other match (3–0) was not against D, for D only had 2 goals scored against them. ∴ B v. C was 3–0, and B did not play D.

∴ D's 2 matches were against A and C. And A did not play C. C's second match (against D) must have been 2–4, and D v. A was ?–0. And since A had 4 goals scored against them, A v. D was 0–4.

Complete solution

A v. B   0–0
A v. D   0–4
B v. C   3–0
C v. D   2–4

Letters for Digits, Two Numbers

$$
\begin{array}{cccc}
& (a) & (b) & (c) \\
& B & Y & B \\
& M & Y & B \\
\hline
& Y & M & M \\
\end{array}
$$

From (c) M is even (B+B). $\therefore$ M = 2, 4, 6 or 8. If B were 5 or more there would be 1 to carry to (b), and we would have (Y+Y+1) which would be odd, and therefore could not be M.

$\therefore$ B is 1, 2, 3 or 4; and Y in (b) is 6, 7, 8 or 9. $\therefore$ there must be 1 to carry from (b) to (a). If B is 1, then M is 2 and Y = 6; but in (a) 1+2+1 = 4 (not 6). If B is 3, then M is 6, and Y = 8. But 3+6+1 = 10 (not possible). If B is 4, then M is 8, and Y = 9. But 4+8+1 = 13 (not possible).

But if B = 2, then M = 4 and Y = 7. And 2+4+1 = 7, and this is right.

Complete solution

$$
\begin{array}{ccc}
2 & 7 & 2 \\
4 & 7 & 2 \\
\hline
7 & 4 & 4 \\
\end{array}
$$

90 The Factory Dinner-Party ★★

Since C does not have A on his right, C must have E on his right (not B or D), and A on his left.

B cannot be next to A, ∴ D is on A's left and B is between D and E.

Thus:

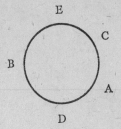

B is between W O and D-S, and B is between E and D; ∴ D is either the W O or D-S, and we are also told that either the D-S or the D-O is D.

∴ D must be D-S. ∴ E is W O. And since the D-O and D-S are not next to each other, C is D-O. A is not B-W, ∴ B is B-W, and A is the Worker.

Complete solution

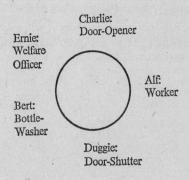

Letters for Digits

```
        d k g b        (a)                - - - -
 d h)g d n s f s       (b)         - -)- - - - - - -
    g g n               (c)                - - -
      s f s             (d)                - - -
      g h k             (e)                - - -
        n f             (f)                  - -
        d h             (g)                  - -
        d g s           (h)                - - -
        d g s           (i)                - - -
```

(The reader is advised to draw a figure like the one on the right above, where the digits can be inserted as they are found.)

Consider the third figures of (b) and (c); n−n is f; ∴ f = 0.
In (g), dh is the divisor; ∴ the third figure in (a) is 1, i.e. g = 1.
Since g = 1, from (d) and (e), s = 2.
From (b), (c) and (d) d−1 = 2, ∴ d = 3.
From (f), (g) and (h) h = 9 and n = 7.
From (d), (e) and (f) k = 5. And b is 312 divided by 39, i.e.
b = 8.

Complete solution

```
          3 5 1 8
3 9 ) 1 3 7 2 0 2
      1 1 7
        2 0 2
        1 9 5
            7 0
            3 9
            3 1 2
            3 1 2
```

92 A Cross Number

1 Down is a perfect square, and from 4 Across it must be the square of an odd number. ∴ it must be the square of 5, 7 or 9. But not 7, for 4 Across would then be 9–9, and this is not possible (see 3 Down). And not 9, for 4 Across would then be 1–1, and this is not possible (see 3 Down). ∴ 1 Down is 25. And 1 Across can only be 234 (see 3 Down and 4 Across).

The last figure of 3 Down is 6, 7, 8 or 9. But not 7 or 8 for 5 Across is a perfect square. And not 6, for 5 Across would then be 16, and the sum of the digits of 2 Down could not be 16. ∴ 5 Across must be 49; and 2 Down must be 394.

Complete solution

¹ 2	² 3	³ 4
⁴ 5	9	5
▨	⁵ 4	9

A Multiplication

$$(a)\ (b)\ (c)\ (d)\ (e)\ (f)$$
$$\begin{array}{cccccc} & P & M & M & T & P \\ & & & & & P \\ \hline N & P & T & R & P & T \end{array}$$

Since P = 2T, P is even. And from (*f*), P times P ends in T (half of P). ∴ P cannot be 2 (2×2 = 4); nor 4 (4×4 ends in 6); nor 6 (6×6 ends in 6). But 8×8 ends in 4 (half of 8), ∴ P = 8, and T = 4.

In (*b*) P = 8, ∴ the first figure of the answer is 6 (8×8 = 64). ∴ N = 6.

Consider (*c*). 8×M must be large enough for 4 to be carried (so that, in (*a*) and (*b*), 64 will become 68). ∴ M must be 5 or 6 (8×5 = 40, and 8×6 = 48). But it cannot be 6, for N = 6; ∴ M = 5.

We now know the whole of the first line. Multiply by 8, and we get the answer.

Complete solution

$$\begin{array}{ccccccc} & 8 & 5 & 5 & 4 & 8 \\ & & & & & 8 \\ \hline 6 & 8 & 4 & 3 & 8 & 4 \end{array}$$

94 Uncle Bungle's Football Puzzle ★★

	Played	Won	Lost	Drawn	Goals for	Goals against
A		2			2	
B			0	0	4	3
C					5	3
D	3					

Consider B. They lost none and drew none, ∴ they won all their matches. But they scored only one goal more than the goals scored against them, so they can only have won one, and ∴ only played one. D played all the other three, ∴ B v. D was 4–3.

Consider A. They won two and scored 2 goals, ∴ the score in each match that they won was 1–0, and they did not play B, for B only played D. So we have:

	A	B	C	D
A			1-0	1-0
B				4-3
C	0-1			
D	0-1	3-4		

And since D played three matches, D played C.
C v. A was 0–1, and C's total goals for and against were 5–3.
∴ C v. D was 5–2.

Complete solution
  A v. C   1–0
  A v. D   1–0
  B v. D   4–3
  C v. D   5–2

95 Addition ★★

Letters for Digits, Two Numbers

(a)	(b)	(c)	(d)	(e)	(f)
R	X	E	K	P	P
R	X	X	R	P	P
H	R	B	H	P	H

Consider (*e*). P must be 0 (0+0 = 0); or 9 (9+9 = 18, and 1 might be carried to make 19).

But if P were 0, then the last figure in the answer (H) should also be 0. ∴ P = 9, and H = 8.

∴ in (*a*) R = 4.

And in (*b*) X = 2; and in (*d*) K = 3. In (*c*) E+2 = B.

∴ E = 5 and B = 7 (the only figures differing by 2 that are left).

Complete solution
  4 2 5 3 9 9
  4 2 2 4 9 9
  8 4 7 8 9 8

96 The Lower the Truer

Since B(1) is true, B is a Pukka or a Shilli-Shalla.

Suppose A(2) true; then B is a Pukka, and B(2) true, and C is a Shilli-Shalla. In this case all three of them make a true statement. But one of them is a Wotta-Woppa. Therefore A(2) is not true, and B is not a Pukka.

∴ B is a Shilli-Shalla, and C is a Pukka (not A, for A(2) is false).

∴ A is a Wotta-Woppa.

B's number is 20 (since B(1) is true), and since 'the lower the truer', A's number is more than 20 and C's number is less. From A(1) (false) C's number is odd. And from C(1) (true) A's number must be 24 or 22 and C's must be 19 or 17. And from C(2) (true) A's number is 22, and C's number is 17.

Complete solution

A is a Wotta-Woppa; his personal number is 22.

B is a Shilli-Shalla; his personal number is 20.

C is a Pukka; his personal number is 17.

97 Cricket

Three Teams

There is no way of getting 3 points, ∴ *A's figure is wrong*.

Each side played two matches, and there is no way of getting 13 points from two matches.

∴ C's figure is wrong.

∴ B's figure is correct.

The only way in which B can get 11 points is by tying one match (5 points) and by winning one on the first innings (6).

Suppose B v. A was a tie; then A get 5 points from their match against B. And A must get at least 2 points from their match against C, making 7 points. But we know that A's incorrect figure of 3 is not more than 2 out. ∴ B v. A was not a tie.

∴ B v. C was a tie and B beat A on the first innings.

∴ A got 2 points from their match against B, and must also have got 2 points from their match against C (making 4 points).

And C got 6 (against A) and 5 (against B) making 11 points.

Complete solution
    A v. B   B won on first innings
    A v. C   C won on first innings
    B v. C   tie

98 Division

Figures All Wrong

```
            3 4      (a)
      1 4 ) 6 1 8    (b)
            5 5      (c)
            ─────
            7 8      (d)
            5 8      (e)
            ─────
```

Since each digit is only 1 out the divisor must start with 2 (it cannot start with 0).

Since the sum comes out exactly, (*d*) and (*e*) must be the same. ∴ they must both start with 6.

∴ the second figure in (a) must be 3 (it cannot be 5 for 2–times 5 is 100 or more).

If the second figure in the divisor was 5 then (d) and (e) would be 75, but they both start with 6. ∴ the divisor must be 23, and (d) and (e) must be 69.

The first figure in (a) cannot be 4, for (c) would then be 92, which it cannot be. ∴ the first figure in (a) is 2, and (c) is 46.

Add up from the bottom and we get:

Complete solution

```
        2 3
   2 3 ) 5 2 9
         4 6
         ───
         6 9
         6 9
         ───

         ───
```

99 A Cross Number

1 Across is even and so is 3 Down.

And since each digit in 3 Down is greater than the one before by the same amount, the first figure in 3 Down must be 2, 4 or 6, and the last figure must be 4, 6 or 8.

Consider 4 Across ('the square of an odd number').
It cannot be 49 or 81 (see 3 Down).
∴ 4 Across must be 25.
∴ 2 Down is 125.
∴ 3 Down is either 456 or 258.
But the last figure of 3 Down cannot be 8 (see 5 Across).
∴ 3 Down is 456.
∴ 5 Across is 256; and 1 Across is 814.

Complete solution

1	2	3
8	1	4
////////	4 2	5
5 2	5	6

100 Football

Four Teams, Old Method

Consider C. 1 goal for and 1 goal against, but no drawn matches.

∴ C can only have played two, and won one (1–0) and lost the other (0–1).

And C cannot have played D, who played only one match but had 3 goals against in this match. ∴ C played A and B.

And since A drew 2, they played all the other three, and their match against D must have been drawn, with a score of 3–3. (Remember that D only played one match, and had 3 goals against.)

B did not play D, but they drew against A and they lost a match.

∴ B v. C was 0–1; ∴ A v. C was 1–0.

B scored 4 goals, ∴ B v. A was 4–4.

Complete solution

    A v. B   4–4
    A v. C   1–0
    A v. D   3–3
    B v. C   0–1

101 The Ladies have a Competition

(i) *Suppose B(2) is true.* Then Clarissa is a Pukka.
∴ C(2) is true, ∴ Agnes is a Shilli-Shalla.
∴ all three of them make a true statement. But this is not possible, for one of them is a Wotta-Woppa.
∴ B(2) is not true. ∴ Clarissa is not a Pukka and Belinda is not a Pukka.
∴ Agnes is a Pukka.
∴ from A(1) Agnes and Angela were first and last (sixth).

(ii) B(1) is false, ∴ Belinda and Beryl are Wotta-Woppas.
∴ Clarissa and Clementine are Shilli-Shallas. ∴ C(1) is true, (for C(2) is not). ∴ Clementine was third.

(iii) A(2) is true, ∴ Beryl was two places higher than Belinda. And since Clementine was third and Agnes and Angela were first and sixth, Beryl must have been second and Belinda fourth. ∴ Clarissa must have been fifth.

Complete solution

Agnes and Angela are Pukkas;
Belinda and Beryl are Wotta-Woppas;
Clarissa and Clementine are Shilli-Shallas.

1 Agnes *or* Angela
2 Beryl
3 Clementine
4 Belinda
5 Clarissa
6 Angela *or* Agnes

Letters for Digits, Three Numbers

	(a)	(b)	(c)	(d)	(e)	(f)
	D	A	R	M	M	M
	P	H	M	P	M	M
	R	M	G	M	M	M
	F	J	K	A	D	D

Consider (e) *and* (f). If M were more than 3, there would be one to carry from (f) and the letter in the answer in (e) would not be D. ∴ M = 1, 2 or 3.

But it cannot be 3, for D would then be 9 and this would make (a) impossible. And if M were 2, then D would be 6, and, in (a), P and R would be at least 1 and 3. (Not 2, for we are assuming M = 2.) But 6+3+1 = 10, and this is not possible.

∴ M = 1, ∴ D = 3, and P and R must be 4 and 2 (but we do not yet know which is which). ∴ F = 9.

From (d) 1+P+1 = A, where P = 2 or 4. But P cannot be 2 for A would then be 4 and either P or R is 4. ∴ P = 4, R = 2 and A = 6.

Consider (b). We know there is nothing to carry to (a) and that H cannot be 1 or 2 or 3. ∴ H = 0. ∴ J must be 7 or 8 (there cannot be more than 1 to carry from (c)).

Suppose J = 8, then G must be 7 (in order that there should be 1 to carry). And K would be 0. But H = 0. ∴ J cannot be 8. ∴ J = 7, G = 5, K = 8.

Complete solution

```
3 6 2 1 1 1
4 0 1 4 1 1
2 1 5 1 1 1
───────────
9 7 8 6 3 3
```

103 Division

Letters for Digits

```
            b h    (a)                  - -
   h f ) m b d     (b)        - - ) - - - -
        m h        (c)                - -
       ─────                         ───
          x d      (d)                - -
          h f      (e)                - -
        ─────                        ───
            f      (f)                  -
        ─────                        ───
```

(The reader is advised to draw a figure, like the one on the right above, and to fill in the digits as they are discovered.)

Since (e) is divisor, h = 1 (see second figure in (a)).

∴ from (d) and (e) x = 2.

∴ in (b) b = 3 (b−1 = 2).

Divisor goes into −1 three times, ∴ divisor must end in 7, ∴ f = 7. ∴ divisor is 17.

$3 \times 17 = 51$, ∴ m = 5.

From (d), (e) and (f) d = 4.

Complete solution

```
          3 1
  1 7 ) 5 3 4
        5 1
      ─────
          2 4
          1 7
        ─────
            7
        ─────
```

104 Multiply by 3

$$
\begin{array}{c}
\text{(a) (b) (c) (d) (e) (f)} \\
\text{L \quad D \quad C \quad F \quad L} \\
\text{3} \\
\hline
\text{H \quad J \quad D \quad H \quad H \quad L}
\end{array}
$$

Consider (f). L×3 produces a number ending in L. ∴ L must be 0 or 5. But it cannot be 0, for in (b) L cannot be 0. ∴ L = 5. ∴ 3×L = 15, ∴ the first figure of the answer must be 1. ∴ H = 1.

∴ in (e) H is 1, and since 1 has been carried from (f) (3×5 = 15), F = 0. And there is nothing to carry to (d). ∴ C = 7 (3×7 = 21) and there is 2 to carry.

(3×D)+2 produces D, ∴ D could be 4 (3×4 = 12, and 2 makes 14), or D could be 9 (3×9 = 27, and 2 makes 29).

But if D were 9, then J would be (5+2), i.e. 7. But we know that C = 7. ∴ D = 4 and J = 6.

Complete solution

$$
\begin{array}{r}
5\ 4\ 7\ 0\ 5 \\
3 \\
\hline
1\ 6\ 4\ 1\ 1\ 5
\end{array}
$$

105 Uncle Bungle Moves to Addition

$$
\begin{array}{cccccc}
(a) & (b) & (c) & (d) & (e) \\
 & 6 & 3 & 2 & 3 \\
 & 9 & 6 & 0 & 6 \\
\hline
2 & 3 & 2 & 5 & 6 \\
\end{array}
$$

Consider (e). If one digit was too large and the other too small we should have $4+5 = 9$, or $2+7 = 9$. But the result of adding cannot be greater than 7. ∴ it must be $2+5 = 7$ (and note that there is not one to carry).

Consider (d). The 0 must become 1, and the 2 must also go up, making $3+1 = 4$ (again note that there is not one to carry).

Consider (c). This can only be $4+7 = 11$ (and note that there is one to carry).

Consider (b). $6+9+1 = 16$. This must be made smaller: $5+8+1 = 14$. And the 2 at the beginning of the last line becomes 1.

Complete solution

$$
\begin{array}{cccc}
 & 5 & 4 & 3 & 2 \\
 & 8 & 7 & 1 & 5 \\
\hline
1 & 4 & 1 & 4 & 7 \\
\end{array}
$$

Football, Three Teams

Since no teams played more than two matches, and since each figure is 1 out, the correct figures must be:

	Played	Won	Lost	Drawn	Goals for	Goals against
A	2	1	0	1	3 or 5	1 or 3
B	1	0	1	0	1 or 3	1 or 3
C	1	0	0	1	2 or 4	0 or 2

Since C drew their only match the score must have been 2–2. Since B lost their only match the score must have been 1–3. And both of these matches must have been against A. These are the only two matches played, ∴ A's goals must be 5 for, 3 against.

Complete solution
   A v. B   3–1
   A v. C   2–2

107 Ring Us!

Suppose B(2) is true. Then C's statements would be true. ∴ A would be a Shilli-Shalla. ∴ A, B and C would all make a true statement. But this is not possible, for one of them is a Wotta-Woppa.

∴ B(2) is not true.

∴ C is a Shilli-Shalla or a Wotta-Woppa.

∴ A must be a Pukka (no one else can be).

∴ A(1) true, ∴ C(2) false.

∴ C is a Wotta-Woppa, ∴ B must be a Shilli-Shalla.

A(2) is true, ∴ B's number is 13. From A(1) C's number is greater than 15, and from B(1) (true) C's number is halfway between A's and B's. And C's number is at least 16. If C's number was 17, then (from B(1)), A's number would be 21. But all the numbers are between 10 and 20.

∴ C's number is 16; and A's number is 19.

Complete solution

A is a Pukka; his telephone number is 19.

B is a Shilli-Shalla; his telephone number is 13.

C is a Wotta-Woppa; his telephone number is 16.

108 A Cross Number

Consider 3 Across and 1 Down. 3 Across cannot be more than 99, ∴ 1 Down cannot be more than 198. If 3 Across started with 90 or less, 1 Down would start with 180 or less, and it would not be possible for the first digit of 3 Across and the second digit of 1 Down to be the same. If 3 Across is 95, 1 Down would be 190. But there are no 0's, ∴ 3 Across is 96 or more.

1 Across is a square of an odd number, and since it starts with 1, it must be the square of 11 or 13. If 11, then the first digit of 2 Down would be 2, and the second digit 6 or more – but this is not possible (see 2 Down), ∴ 1 Across is the square of 13 (169) and 2 Down can only be 678.

∴ since 3 Across is 97, 1 Down is 194.

∴ 4 Across is 484.

Complete solution

1	2	
1	6	9
3 9	7	////
4 4	8	4

109 Addition

Letters for Digits, Two Numbers

	(a)	(b)	(c)	(d)	(e)	(f)	(g)	(h)	(i)
	Y	A	B	A	E	W	T	P	
	Y	A	W	H	P	T	T	H	
	J	P	K	P	J	E	Y	A	H

The first figure in the answer must be 1. ∴ J = 1.

Consider (i). P+H = H. ∴ P = 0. ∴ since the first two figures of the answer are 10, Y = 5.

Consider (g). Y = 5, and since P = 0 there cannot be anything to carry on to the next line (E+0 = E). ∴ W and T are both less than 5, ∴ in (h) T+T is less than 10. ∴ W+T

276

= 5. Neither of them can be 1, for J = 1; ∴ one of them is 2 and the other 3 (but we cannot yet say which is which).

Consider (c). We know that there is nothing to carry, and that A is not 1, 2, or 3, ∴ A = 4.
∴ from (h) T = 2, ∴ W = 3.
From (e) H = 7, and there is one to carry. ∴ in (d) B must be 6. ∴ there is one to carry on to (c), ∴ K = 9. ∴ by elimination, E = 8.

Complete solution

```
    5 4 6 4 8 3 2 0
    5 4 3 7 0 2 2 7
  ─────────────────
  1 0 9 0 1 8 5 4 7
```

110 Division   ★★

Some Missing Figures

```
                  - 7 -      (a)
     - -)- - - - 1           (b)
        - - 4                (c)
      ───────
        - - -                (d)
        - -                  (e)
      ───────
        - -                  (f)
        - -                  (g)
      ───────
```

(e) is the divisor times 7, and when subtracted from – – – it leaves only one figure. ∴ (e) must be at least 91.

The divisor cannot be as much as 15, for $7 \times 15 = 105$. And since (f) and (g) end in 1 (last figure of (b)), ∴ divisor is odd. ∴ it must be 13 (not 11 for 11×9 is only 99 and there are three figures in (c)).

∴ (c) must be $13 \times 8 (= 104)$.
And since (f) and (g) end in 1, they must be 91.

Add up from the bottom and we get:

Complete solution

```
              8 7 7
      13)1 1 4 0 1
         1 0 4
         ─────
           1 0 0
             9 1
           ─────
               9 1
               9 1
             ─────
```

111 Right or Wrong?

(i) *Let us first assume that all statements are true.*
From B's statement, B was second or third.
From E's statement, A was higher than B; and from A's statement C was higher than A.
∴ the first three must be C, A, B in that order.
From C's statement, D was higher than E.
∴ the order is:

1	C
2	A
3	B
4	D
5	E

(ii) *Assume now that all statements are false.*
From D's statement, D was first, second or third, but from C's statement, E was higher than D, ∴ D was second or third, and E was first or second.

From B's statement, B was first, fourth or fifth; but, from E's statement, B was not fifth; and, from A's statement, A was not fifth, ∴ B was not fourth. ∴ B was first.

∴ E was second, and D was third. And from A's statement, A was fourth and C was fifth.

Complete solution

	(i)			(ii)	
	1	Charlie		1	Bert
	2	Alf		2	Ernie
	3	Bert		3	Duggie
	4	Duggie		4	Alf
	5	Ernie		5	Charlie

112 Football   ★★

Four Teams, Old Method

Consider C. They lost one, and since only 1 goal was scored against them, the score in this match was 0–1. They only played two, ∴ the score in their other match was 3–0.

Consider B. After drawing two matches they must have as many goals for as against, ∴ they cannot have played a third match, for this would have made their goals for more or less than the goals scored against them.

∴ B only played two (and drew both); ∴ B did not play C.

∴ C's two matches were against A and D.

And B's two matches were against A and D.

A only played two, ∴ A did not play D.

The score in C's two matches was 3–0 and 0–1, but D only had 2 goals against them. ∴ C v. D was 0–1; and C v. A was 3–0.

D's other match against B was drawn. ∴ the score was 2–2.

∴ B v. A was 3–3.

Complete solution

A v. B   3–3
A v. C   0–3
B v. D   2–2
C v. D   0–1

113 Cricket

Three Teams

A gets 12 points from two matches. They must either get 6 points from each match (wins on first innings), or they must win one (10 points) and get 2 points from the other for a drawn match.

Suppose that they get 6 points from each match. Then C gets 2 points from the match with A, ∴ C gets 8 points from the match with B. But there is no way of getting 8 points from a match. ∴ our assumption is wrong, and A's 12 points must be 10 for a win and 2 for a draw.

Suppose that A v. B was a win (10 points), and A v. C 2 points. Then C gets 6 points from the match against A, and must therefore get 4 points from the match against B, so that B gets 4 points too (a tie on first innings). ∴ B gets only 4 points – but we know that B got 6 points.

∴ our assumption is wrong, ∴ A v. C was a win.

∴ A got 2 points against B, ∴ B got 6 points against A, and no points against C, ∴ C won against B.

Complete solution

A v. B   B won on first innings;
A v. C   A won;
B v. C   C won.

114 Letters for Digits

A Multiplication

$$
\begin{array}{cccc}
(a) & (b) & (c) & (d) \\
W & V & G & E \\
 & & & W \\
\hline
T & F & E & W \\
\end{array}
$$

We know that W is odd. Suppose that W was 5; then since the first digit of (*a*) is 5, and $5 \times 5 = 25$, ∴ there would be 5 digits in the answer, not 4. ∴ W is less than 5. It cannot be 1, for the answer would then be the same as the number to be multiplied, ∴ W = 3.

And since the last figure of the answer is also W, E = 1, and there is nothing to carry to (*c*). ∴ from (*c*), 3 times G ends in 1, ∴ G = 7, and since $3 \times 7 = 21$, there is 2 to carry.

Since $3 \times 3 = 9$, T = 9, and 3 times V must be at least 2 less than 10. We know that there are no 0's. And V cannot be 1, for E is 1. ∴ V = 2, and F = 8.

Complete solution

$$
\begin{array}{cccc}
3 & 2 & 7 & 1 \\
 & & & 3 \\
\hline
9 & 8 & 1 & 3 \\
\end{array}
$$

115 C was Silent

Suppose B's statement is true, then D is a Pukka and his statements are true. ∴ A is also a Pukka, and his statements are true. ∴ A and D are Pukkas, and one of the other two is a Shilli-Shalla and the other a Wotta-Woppa.

But A's statement cannot be true (C cannot be more truthful than D who according to our assumption is a Pukka). ∴ our assumption is wrong. ∴ D is not a Pukka and since B has made a false remark, B is not a Pukka either. ∴ A and C must be the Pukkas.

But D's remark is true (A is a Pukka), ∴ D must be the Shilli-Shalla and B must be the Wotta-Woppa.

Complete solution

A   is a Pukka;
B   is a Wotta-Woppa;
C   is a Pukka;
D   is a Shilli-Shalla.

116 A Cross Number

5 Across is a perfect square, and from 4 Down and 2 Down both the digits are even. Two-figure perfect squares are 16, 25, 36, 49, 64 and 81. But the only one with both digits even is 64, ∴ 5 Across is 64.

4 Down is a multiple of 11, ∴ it must be 66. ∴ 3 Across is 468 and 2 Down is 984.

Sum of digits of 1 Across is 11, ∴ it is 119. And 1 Down is 141.

Complete solution

¹ 1	1	² 9
³ 4	⁴ 6	8
1	⁵ 6	4

117 Addition

Letters for Digits, Three Numbers

$$
\begin{array}{cccccc}
(a) & (b) & (c) & (d) & (e) & (f) \\
Y & R & R & M & & P \\
Y & R & P & M & & P \\
Y & R & Y & M & & P \\
\hline
R & Y & M & A & B & P \\
\end{array}
$$

Consider (*f*). P must be 0 or 5.

The most that can be carried when three digits are added together is 2 (9+9+9 = 27).

∴ R = 1 or 2.

∴ R+R+R cannot be more than 6. ∴ there is nothing to carry from (*c*) to (*b*). ∴ Y must be 5 and R = 1.

And since Y = 5, ∴ P = 0.

Consider (*d*). We know that R = 1, P = 0 and Y = 5.

∴ there is nothing to carry, ∴ M = 3.

∴ from (*e*) B = M+M+M = 9 (and there is nothing to carry to (*d*)).

∴ A = R+P+Y = 6.

Complete solution

$$
\begin{array}{r}
5\ 1\ 1\ 3\ 0 \\
5\ 1\ 0\ 3\ 0 \\
5\ 1\ 5\ 3\ 0 \\
\hline
1\ 5\ 3\ 6\ 9\ 0 \\
\end{array}
$$

118 Uncle Bungle Passes through a Bad Patch

```
              – 2       (a)
     5 –)5 – – –         (b)
          – – –          (c)
          ‾‾‾‾‾
            – –          (d)
          – 9            (e)
```

If divisor is 5– then the second figure in (a) cannot be 2, for 2 times 5– comes to more than 100. If the second figure in (a) is 2, then the second figure in (e) cannot be 9. ∴ either 5 in divisor or 2 in (a) is wrong, and either 9 in (e) or 2 in (a) is wrong. But only one figure is wrong, so it must be 2 in (a). ∴ all the other figures are right, ∴ the divisor is 59, and the second figure in (a) should be 1.

Since 59×8 is only 472, (c) must be 59×9, i.e. 531.

Add up from the bottom and we have:

Complete solution

```
              9 1
     5 9)5 3 6 9
        5 3 1
        ‾‾‾‾‾
            5 9
            5 9
            ‾‾‾
```

119 Football

Four Teams, Old Method

Consider the drawn matches. B got no points, ∴ drew none.
And we know that D drew none, ∴ A's drawn match must
have been against C. And since A scored no goals, A v. C
was 0–0.

D got 4 points and, since they lost none and drew none,
they won two (each by a single goal), and these two matches
were against A and B.

Since A only played two, they did not play B. And since
A scored no goals, A v. D was 0–1. (D won two matches,
each by a single goal.) ∴ from D's goals for and against
D v. B was 3–2.

Complete solution

  A v. C 0–0
  A v. D 0–1
  B v. D 2–3

We know that B(2) is true; suppose C(1) is also true, then A, B and C all make at least one true statement. But this is not possible.

∴ C(1) cannot be true, ∴ A is not a Pukka. And since C has made a false statement, ∴ C is not a Pukka; ∴ B is a Pukka. ∴ C(2) cannot be true (B must be older than A). ∴ C is a Wotta-Woppa and A is a Shilli-Shalla.

From B(1) (true), A is 6 years older than C. ∴ A(1) ('B is 7 years older than A') cannot be true, for this would make B 13 years older than C, but the difference between the oldest and youngest cannot be more than 12.

∴ A(2) must be true (A is a Shilli-Shalla).

∴ B is 26 or less, ∴ from B(1) A must be 25, and C must be 19.

Complete solution

A is a Shilli-Shalla, and is 25;
B is a Pukka, and is 26;
C is a Wotta-Woppa, and is 19.

121 Two of One and One of the Other Two

Suppose B's statement is true. Then A is a Pukka, and since A's statement is true, ∴ D is also a Pukka.

∴ D's statement is true, and B is a Wotta-Woppa.

But this does not agree with our original assumption that B's statement was true.

∴ B's statement is not true, and ∴ B could be a Shilli-Shalla or a Wotta-Woppa.

Since B's statement is not true, ∴ A is not a Pukka. ∴ A is a Shilli-Shalla or a Wotta-Woppa.

   If C's statement is true then C is a Wotta-Woppa (who make *no* true statements).

∴ C's statement is not true.

∴ D is a Pukka (no one else can be); ∴ his statement is true and B is a Wotta-Woppa.

A cannot be a Wotta-Woppa, for his statement is true. ∴ A is a Shilli-Shalla.

C cannot be more truthful than A, for he has made a false statement.

∴ C must belong to a tribe that is as truthful as A's.

∴ C is a Shilli-Shalla.

Complete solution

   A is a Shilli-Shalla;
   B is a Wotta-Woppa;
   C is a Shilli-Shalla;
   D is a Pukka.

```
(a) (b) (c) (d) (e) (f) (g)
 X  Q  R  X  F  X  A
                      5
─────────────────────────
 A  M  Q  K  D  F  Q
```

If X were 2, there would be another figure in the answer $(5 \times 2 = 10)$. $\therefore$ X = 1.

When a number is multiplied by 5 the result ends in 0 or in 5. $\therefore$ in (g) Q is 0 or 5.

Suppose Q = 0. Then, in (b), Q is 0, $\therefore$ there can be nothing to carry to (a), $\therefore$ A would be 5 (for X = 1). But if, in (g), A is 5, then Q would also be 5.

$\therefore$ our assumption is wrong, and Q = 5, not 0.

Consider (a). $5 \times 1 = 5$, and 2 is carried from (b). $\therefore$ A = 7. $\therefore$ the last two digits in the | answer are 85 (17 × 5), and F = 8. $\therefore$ in (e) $5 \times 8 = 40$, and since there is nothing to carry D = 0. Since there is 4 to carry to (d) K = 9 (5+4), and there is nothing to carry to (c). $\therefore$ in (c) R must be odd (5 times an even number ends in 0). But the only odd number left is 3. $\therefore$ R = 3. And M = 6 (5+1).

Complete solution
```
 1 5 3 1 8 1 7
             5
───────────────
 7 6 5 9 0 8 5
```

123 Uncle Bungle gets 'One in Three' Wrong

```
              7 –      (a)
      – 5 )– – –       (b)
          – –          (c)
          ———
          – – –        (d)
          – – 8        (e)
```

Look first for figure that is wrong. If divisor were 15 (and it cannot be less) then (c) would be $15 \times 7 = 105$. But this is not possible for (c) has two figures.

∴ either the 5 or the 7 is wrong.

If divisor ends in 5, then (e) cannot end in 8. ∴ either the 5 or the 8 is wrong.

But we know that only one figure is wrong, ∴ it must be the 5 in divisor. And 7 and 8 are correct.

(c) is the divisor times 7. ∴ the divisor is 14 or less ($14 \times 7 = 98$). But if (c) were 98 or 91 (13×7), there would not be a first figure for (d).

And if divisor were 11, then since $11 \times 9 = 99$, there would not be three figures in (d).

∴ divisor is 12, (c) is 84, and (d) and (e) are 108 (12×9).

Add up from the bottom and we get:

Complete solution

```
            7 9
    1 2 )9 4 8
        8 4
        ———
        1 0 8
        1 0 8
```

124 A Cross Number

The second digit of 5 Across is even, ∴ the third digit of 3 Down is even.

∴ all digits of 3 Down are even ('each digit is 2 greater than one before').

∴ last digit of 3 Down must be 6 or 8 (not 4 for 3 Down would then be 024). But it cannot be 6, for the last digit of 1 Across would then be 2, but no perfect square ends in 2.

∴ 3 Down is 468 and 5 Across is 38.

The first digit of 4 Across must be 6. ∴ 1 Down ('A perfect square') is either 16 or 36. Suppose it is 36: then 1 Across must be 324 (18 squared). And 2 Down would be 2–3. But the sum of the digits of 2 Down is 16, and this is not possible (the second digit would have to be 11).

∴ 1 Down must be 16 (not 36).

And 1 Across (a perfect square) is 1–4, ∴ 144.

∴ 2 Down is 493.

Complete solution

1	2	3
1	4	4
4 6	9	. 6
/////////	5 3	8

Letters for Digits, Two Numbers

	(a)	(b)	(c)	(d)	(e)
	X	J	D	F	C
	C	D	F	C	C
	J	J	J	Y	J

From (e) J is even (C+C). ∴ in (a) X = C−1, and there must be 1 to carry from the second line down. In (b) (J+D) cannot equal (10+J), ∴ there is 1 to carry from (c), and D = 9. J cannot be 2, for in (a) C would then be 1 and X would be 0. But it does not make sense to have 0 in (a).

If J were 8, then (b) would be 8+9+1 (carried) = 18. And F in (c) would have to be either 8 or 9. But D = 9, and we are assuming that J is 8. ∴ J cannot be 8.

Suppose J = 6. Then we have:

$$
\begin{array}{r}
2\ 6\ 9\ 7\ 3 \\
3\ 9\ 7\ 3\ 3 \\
\hline
6\ 6\ 6\ -\ 6
\end{array}
$$

And (d) would end in 0, and there would be 1 to carry. But there cannot be 1 to carry (9+7 = 16).

∴ our assumption is wrong. ∴ J must be 4.

∴ C = 2, X = 1, F = 5 and Y = 7.

Complete solution

$$
\begin{array}{r}
1\ 4\ 9\ 5\ 2 \\
2\ 9\ 5\ 2\ 2 \\
\hline
4\ 4\ 4\ 7\ 4
\end{array}
$$

126 Bert was not First

Since C was as many places below F as B was above A, and the difference between C and F was more than 1,

∴ F and B cannot be fifth or sixth; and C and A cannot be first or second.

We also know that B was not first, F was not fourth and neither A nor C was sixth.

∴ the possibilities are:

1			D	E	F
2		B	D	E	F
3	A	B	C	D	E	F
4	A	B	C	D	E
5	A		C	D	E
6			D	E

We also know that the number of D's place was half the number of E's.

∴ D was first, second or third, and E was second, fourth or sixth.

∴ D was not sixth, ∴ E was sixth, ∴ D was third.

∴ F was first (no one else can be). ∴ B was second (no one else can be).

And since F is as many places above C as B is above A,

∴ C must be fourth and A must be fifth.

Complete solution

1. Fred
2. Bert
3. Duggie
4. Charlie
5. Alf
6. Ernie

Five Teams, Old Method

Since the total of goals for must be the same as the total of the goals against, ∴ B scored no goals. C played two and lost one, and had 7 goals for and 4 against. ∴ C must have won their other game.

Neither A, D nor E drew any, ∴ no match was drawn. And since B cannot have won any (they scored no goals), ∴ B played only one match and the score was 0–5. Neither A nor D scored as many as 5 goals, and though E scored 5 they could not all have been against B for they won 2 matches. ∴ B's match was against C and the score was 0–5.

C only played two, ∴ C lost their other match 2–4. ∴ C's other match was against E (the only other team that scored as many as 4 goals).

∴ C v. E was 2–4. And we have:

	A	B	C	D	E
A					
B			0-5		
C		5-0			2-4
D					
E			4-2		

D won one match and their goals were 2–2, ∴ they must have lost one (we know that they cannot have played more than two).

∴ D played A and E, and since E had 5 goals for and 3 against, this leaves 1–0 for E's other match or matches. But since there were no draws, E can only have played one other match.

∴ E v. D was 1–0, D v. A was 2–1, and E did not play A.

Complete solution
  A v. D   1–2
  B v. C   0–5
  C v. E   2–4
  D v. E   0–1

128 Some More Wrong Addition   ★★★

	(a)	(b)	(c)	(d)
	7	6	6	8
	2	6	9	2
	9	0	2	7

Look first at (d). If we put 8 up by 1 and 2 down by 1 we shall get 10, which will not do. Clearly we must put them both down: $7+1 = 8$. (Note that there is not 1 to carry.)

Consider (c). The 9 can only become 8. If 6 became 7 we should have $7+8 = 15$, which will not do. ∴ it must be $5+8 = 13$ (note that there is 1 to carry).

Consider (b). The 0 can only become 1. Clearly both 6's must become 5, and we have $5+5+1 = 11$ (note that there is again 1 to carry).

Consider (a). The 9 can only be 8. ∴ $7+2$ is going to be too big, and remember that there is 1 to carry from the next line. ∴ we have $6+1+1 = 8$.

294

Complete solution

```
  6 5 5 7
  1 5 8 1
  ───────
  8 1 3 8
```

129 Division   ★★★

Letters for Digits

```
           k n m d      (a)              - - - -
  h e ) e n d j n        (b)      - - ) - - - - -
      c g                (c)              - -
      ─────
        k d              (d)              - -
        d k              (e)              - -
        ─────
          p j            (f)              - -
          g m            (g)              - -
          ─────
            m n          (h)              - -
            m h          (i)              - -
            ─────
              h          (j)               -
```

(The reader is advised to draw a figure, like the one on the right above, where the digits can be inserted as they are found.)

(*c*), (*e*), (*g*) and (*i*) are the divisor multiplied by four different figures none of which is 1. If the divisor started with 2, one of these multiples would be at least 100. ∴ divisor must start with 1, ∴ h = 1. ∴ from (*h*), (*i*) and (*j*) n = 2. (*e*) is 1– multiplied by 2 (the second figure of (*a*)), ∴ d = 3 (it cannot be 2), ∴ in (*d*) k = 4. From (*d*), (*e*) and (*f*) p = 9, ∴ in (*g*) g = 8. (*e*), 34, is the divisor multiplied by 2, ∴ e = 7, ∴ in (*c*) c = 6.

295

The only figures left are 0 and 5. From (*h*) and (*i*) m = 5, ∴
j = 0.

Complete solution

```
            4 2 5 3
   1 7 ) 7 2 3 0 2
         6 8
         ‾‾‾
           4 3
           3 4
           ‾‾‾
             9 0
             8 5
             ‾‾‾
               5 2
               5 1
               ‾‾‾
                 1
```

130 Cricket

Four Teams

A must have 20 points from two wins, and 5 points for a ti◄
(there is no other possibility). But B cannot have tied an◄
(only 2 points); and C cannot have tied any (if C had go◄
5 points for a tie there is no way in which they could hav◄
got their other 3 points)
∴ A v. D was a tie and A must have won their other tw◄
matches against B and against C.

So we have:

	A	B	C	D
A		10	10	5
B	0			
C	0			
D	5			

B cannot have lost their match against C, for C would then have got 10 points. But C only got 8. ∴ B got their 2 points from their match against C, and D beat B. C v. D was a win on the first innings for D (6 points for D and 2 for C).

Complete solution

A v. B   A won
A v. C   A won
A v. D   tie
B v. C   C won on first innings
B v. D   D won
C v. D   D won on first innings

131 Division

Some Missing Figures

```
              - - -        (a)
      - -)- - - - 5        (b)
          - 0              (c)
          ___
          - - -            (d)
         4 - -             (e)
         ___
              - -          (f)
              - -          (g)
```

Since (c) ends in 0, ∴ the divisor must end in 0, 5 or an even number. But since (f) and (g) end in 5 (brought down from (b)), ∴ the divisor cannot end in 0 or an even number, but must end in 5.

Since (c) and (g) are different two-figure multiples of the divisor, the divisor must be under 50.

$35 \times 9 = 315$, but (e) starts with 4, ∴ the divisor must be 45 and (e) is $45 \times 9 = 405$. (c) must be 90, and (f) and (g) must be 45.

Add up from the bottom and we get:

Complete solution

```
              2 9 1
      4 5)1 3 0 9 5
          9 0
          ___
          4 0 9
          4 0 5
          _____
              4 5
              4 5
              ___
```

132 Addition

Letters for Digits, Three Numbers

```
(a) (b) (c) (d) (e) (f) (g)
 G  G  J  D  G  F  F
 G  G  G  P  B  F  F
 G  G  B  D  G  F  F
────────────────────
 Z  N  Y  H  P  B  G
```

G must be 1, 2 or 3 (if it were 4 or more there would be another letter before Z in the answer).

If G = 3, then from (g) F would be 1, ∴ B would also be 3. ∴ G is not 3.

If G = 1, then F = 7 (7+7+7 = 21), and B in (f) would be 3 but Z = 3 (1+1+1) and B and Z cannot be the same. ∴ G is not 1 ∴ G = 2, and F = 4 (4+4+4 = 12), and from (f) B = 3. From (a) Z = 6, and from (b) N = 7 (there cannot be more than 1 to carry from (c)).

From (e) P = 2+3+2+1 (that has been carried) = 8. From (d) D+8+D = H, ∴ H = 0 or is even. But we know what 2, 4, 6 and 8 are, ∴ H = 0, ∴ D = 1 (and there is 1 to carry). The only digits left are 5 and 9. ∴ J = 9 and Y = 5.

Complete solution
```
2 2 9 1 2 4 4
2 2 2 8 3 4 4
2 2 3 1 2 4 4
─────────────
6 7 5 0 8 3 2
```

133 A Cross Number

4 Down (two figures) is the square root of 5 Across (three figures), ∴ 4 Down must be less than 32 ($32^2 = 1024$). But the first figure of 4 Down cannot be 1 or 3 (3 Across is even). ∴ 4 Down is 2–.

And the second figure of 4 Down must be the same when squared, ∴ it must be 1, 5 or 6. But not 1, for the second digit of 4 Down is greater than the first.

∴ 4 Down is 25 or 26, and 5 Across is 625 or 676.

But the second figure of 5 Across cannot be 2 (see 2 Down).

∴ 5 Across is 676 and 4 Down is 26. And 2 Down is 357.

∴ 1 Across is 13 (5 Across is $2 \times 2 \times 13 \times 13$).

And 1 Down is 186.

Complete solution

¹ 1	² 3	▨
³ 8	5	⁴ 2
⁵ 6	7	6

134 Football

Four Teams, New Method

Four matches have been played (six minus the two that have not been played).

∴ 40 points were given for wins or draws.

∴ C must have 30, and must have won all their matches.

300

And A and B must have got 5 each, ∴ A v. B was a draw.
And D only played one match (against C).

So we have:

	A	B	C	D
A	✕	dr.	l.	✕
B	dr.	✕	l.	✕
C	w.	w.	✕	w.
D	✕	✕	l.	✕

∴ D got 3 goals against C. ∴ the score was 3–4 (not more than 7 goals were scored in any match).
A got 5 points for a draw, ∴ scored 2 goals.
∴ A v. B was 1–1; and A v. C was 1–?.

B got 5 points for a draw, ∴ scored 3 goals. ∴ B v. C was 2–?. C scored 9 goals, four of them against D, and since they won all their matches, C v. A was 2–1; and C v. B was 3–2.

Complete solution
A v. B   1–1
A v. C   1–2
B v. C   2–3
C v. D   4–3

Suppose C(1) is true. Then B is a Pukka, and ∴ B(1) is true, so that the Door-Shutter is a Wotta-Woppa.

Since, according to our assumption C and B both make true remarks, A is the Wotta-Woppa. ∴ A's statements are false. ∴ A(2) is false, and A (who is the Wotta-Woppa) is not the Door-Shutter.

But this contradicts B(1), ∴ our original assumption must be false. ∴ B is not a Pukka, and, since C has made a false statement, A is the Pukka. ∴ A(1) is true, and since C is more truthful than B, ∴ C is the Shilli-Shalla, and B is the Wotta-Woppa.

∴ From A(2), A is the Door-Shutter.

From C(2) (true) C is not the Door-Opener, ∴ B is the Door-Opener, ∴ C must be the Door-Knob-Polisher.

Complete solution

Alf is a Pukka and is the Door-Shutter;

Bert is a Wotta-Woppa and is the Door-Opener;

Charlie is a Shilli-Shalla and is the Door-Knob-Polisher.

136 Division ★★★

Letters for Digits

b q g	(a)	`- - -`
h v) g h q h	(b)	`- - ) - - - -`
p b	(c)	`- -`
p q	(d)	`- -`
m q	(e)	`- -`
h e h	(f)	`- - -`
v p g	(g)	`- - -`
v q	(h)	`- -`

(The reader is advised to draw a figure, like the one on the right above, and to fill in the digits there as they are discovered.)

From (d), (e) and (f) e = 0.

In (c), hv multiplied by b ends in b.

In (e), hv multiplied by q ends in q.

In (g), hv multiplied by g ends in g.

∴ v must be 1 (1 multiplied by any number ends in the same number).

∴ from (f) and (g) h = 2.

In (g), g must be greater than 2, ∴ there is one to borrow, ∴ p = 8.

∴ in (b), g = 9, ∴ in (h), q = 3, ∴ in (e), m = 6. And in (c), b = 4.

Complete solution

```
           4 3 9
    2 1 ) 9 2 3 2
          8 4
          ‾‾‾
            8 3
            6 3
            ‾‾‾
            2 0 2
            1 8 9
            ‾‾‾‾‾
              1 3
```

137 Our Factory – Logic and Charm

Read through (1), (2), (3) and (4) carefully and you will see that the information given about logic and charm is as follows:

Order	Logic					Charm				
1					C					A
2	B			A	C	D			C	A
3	B	D	E	A	C	D	B		C	A
4		D	E	A	C	D	B	E	C	A
5		D		A			B		C	

C is first in logic, and A is first in charm (no one else can be).

Charm. E is fourth (the only possible place).

And since E is below B, B is third.

∴ C is fifth (no one else can be). ∴ D is second (the only place left).

Logic. If E were third, then B would be second, and D would be fourth or fifth. But B is only one place above D (see (1), and see order for charm).

∴ E must be fourth, B second and D third.

∴ A is fifth.

Complete solution

	Logic	Charm
1	Charlie	Alf
2	Bert	Duggie
3	Duggie	Bert
4	Ernie	Ernie
5	Alf	Charlie

138 Addition

Letters for Digits, Four Numbers

(a)	(b)	(c)	(d)	(e)
P	P	R	P	
P	P	C	C	
P	R	R	P	
P	C	X	C	
R	R	A	Q	R

The most that can be carried when four digits are added together is 3. ∴ R is 1, 2 or 3. But from (e) R must be even (P+C+P+C). ∴ R = 2.

∴ in (*b*), P = 5, and there are 2 to carry from (*c*) to (*b*).

In (*e*) C must be 1 or 6 (5+1+5+1 = 12; 5+6+5+6 = 22). Suppose C is 1. Then (*c*) would be (5+5+2+1), and it would not then be possible for 2 to be carried to (*b*). ∴ C must be 6.

(*c*) now adds up to 18, and since there cannot be more than 2 to carry from (*d*) (2+6+2+X), A must be 0. And since Q cannot now be 0, Q = 1 and X = 9.

Complete solution

```
    5 5 2 5
    5 5 6 6
    5 2 2 5
    5 6 9 6
  ─────────
  2 2 0 1 2
```

139 Bungle Blunders

```
            8 -      (a)
  - 2 ) - - 6        (b)
        - 5          (c)
      ─────
        - -          (d)
        - -          (e)
```

Look first for the figure that is wrong. The divisor and (*c*) cannot both be right, for no multiple of –2 can end in 5.

And if 8 is correct then (*c*) would be even.

∴ either 8 or 5 is wrong.

But only one figure is wrong; ∴ 5 is wrong, and the other three figures are correct.

∴ (*c*) is (–2×8), and this can only be 96.

And the divisor is 12.

(d) and (e) end in 6, and must therefore be either 96 or 36. But if (d) were 96, there would have to be an extra figure at the beginning of (b) ∴ (d) and (e) are 36.

Add up from the bottom and we get:

Complete solution

```
        8 3
  1 2 )9 9 6
      9 6
      ───
        3 6
        3 6
        ───
```

140 Half of them are Wotta-Woppas

Suppose B's statement is true. Then A and B must between them be the Pukka and the Shilli-Shalla, and the other two must both be Wotta-Woppas.

∴ C's statement ('D is a Wotta-Woppa') must be true, but it can't be for C is a Wotta-Woppa.

∴ our assumption was wrong, and B's statement cannot be true.

∴ A's statement ('B is a Pukka') is also false, and D's statement ('A is a Pukka') is also false.

∴ C's statement must be true for he is the only person who can be a Pukka.

And from B's statement (which we know to be false) A does not belong to a more truthful tribe than D, ∴ since D is a Wotta-Woppa, A must also be a Wotta-Woppa (belonging to a tribe that is as truthful, but not more), and B must be a Shilli-Shalla.

Complete solution

A   is a Wotta-Woppa;
B   is a Shilli-Shalla;
C   is a Pukka;
D   is a Wotta-Woppa.

141 Football

Four Teams, Old Method

A won none, and drew none. And their goals for were only 1 less than goals against.

∴ A only played one, and they lost it (2–3).

They cannot have played B, for B only had 1 goal against. And they cannot have played D, for D won none. ∴ A played C, and the score was 2–3.

We know that C only played two matches, and their other match was a draw against D. (For we know that D drew one, and it can only have been against C.) And since C scored 4 goals, C v. D was 1–1. D had 5 goals against, ∴ they must have played another match, against B, for we know that they did not play A. ∴ D v. B was ?–4.

And since B had 1 goal against, and this was their only match (for there is no one else they could have played), D v. B was 1–4.

Complete solution

A v. C   2–3
B v. D   4–1
C v. D   1–1

Figures All Wrong

```
              8 3    (a)
      9 2 ) 7 0 2 6  (b)
          6 6 0      (c)
          ─────
            2 2 4    (d)
            1 0 2    (e)
            ─────
```

The second figure of (*a*) must be 2 or 4. Suppose it is 2. Then since $99 \times 2 = 198$, (*e*) would start with 1. But as it does, and we know that all the figures are wrong, the second figure in (*a*) must be 4, not 2.

The divisor cannot end in 0, for in that case every multiple of it would end in 0, and (*c*) does end in 0.

The last figures in (*b*), (*d*) and (*e*) (which must all be the same in the correct sum) are even. But not 6, 4 or 2 (the figures given), ∴ 8.

And the divisor must end in 2 or 7 ($4 \times 2 = 8$; $4 \times 7 = 28$). But not 2, for this is the figure given. ∴ the divisor is –7. The divisor cannot start with 9 (the figure given). ∴ the most it can be is 87.

Suppose it was 77, then (*d*) and (*e*) would be $77 \times 4 = 308$. But the second figure in (*e*) is given as 0, ∴ not 77. And if the divisor were 67 or less, (*d*) and (*e*) would start with 1 or 2, which are the figures given, or would only have two figures. ∴ the divisor can only be 87.

$87 \times 7 = 609$, but 6 is the figure given in (*c*) ∴ (*a*) must be 94.

Complete solution

```
            9 4
    8 7 ) 8 1 7 8
        7 8 3
        ─────
          3 4 8
          3 4 8
          ─────
```

143 Cricket

Five Teams

(i) No one can play more than four matches. Since B got 35 points they must have played four, won three (30 points) and tied one (5 points). B's tied match was not against E (only 2 points) and not against A (6 points and they cannot be 5+1). We know that D (12 points) won one of their matches, ∴ they cannot have tied with B, for they would then have got at least 15 points. ∴ B's tied match was against C, and they won the other three.

(ii) D won one match. Not against B (who lost none); not against A (who only played two, losing one against B and scoring 6 points from the other); and not against C (who tied with B and got 6 points from the other match they played). ∴ D must have won against E.

(iii) A's second match was a win on the first innings, and C's second match was a win on the first innings. ∴ A did not play C.

(iv) E got 2 points; this can only have been in their match against A. ∴ A v. E was a win on the first innings for A. And since A only played two, A did not play D. And C's other match was a win on the first innings against D.

Complete solution
    A v. B   B won
    A v. E   A won on first innings
    B v. C   tie
    B v. D   B won
    B v. E   B won
    C v. D   C won on first innings
    D v. E   D won

144 Addition

Letters for Digits, Three Numbers

	(a)	(b)	(c)	(d)	(e)	(f)	(g)	(h)
	B	Y	T	Z	B	X	D	D
	B	S	V	Z	D	B	D	D
	B	B	S	Z	D	B	D	D
	X	V	N	P	P	N	B	B

Since in (a) B+B+B is less than 10, ∴ B = 1, 2 or 3.

Suppose B was 1. Then from (h) D would have to be 7 (7+7+7 = 21), ∴ in (g) (7+7+7+2) would be 23. ∴ B is not 1.

Suppose B was 2. Then from (h) D would have to be 4 (4+4+4 = 12), ∴ in (g) (4+4+4+1) would be 13. ∴ B is not 2.

∴ B = 3, ∴ D = 1 and X = 9. And from (f) N = 5 (9+3+3 = 15, and there is one to carry).

From (e) P = 6 (3+1+1+1 = 6). From (d) Z+Z+Z = 6, ∴ Z = 2. From (c) T+V+S = 15 (not 5, for the only two digits left which are less than 5 are 0 and 4; and not 25, for the three largest digits left are 8, 7 and 4 which add up to 19). It is easy to see that T, V and S must be 0, 7 and 8, but we cannot yet say which is which.

∴ in (b) Y = 4, and since there is nothing to carry to (a), ∴ S = 0, V = 8 and T = 7.

Complete solution

```
3 4 7 2 3 9 1 1
3 0 8 2 1 3 1 1
3 3 0 2 1 3 1 1
―――――――――――――――
9 8 5 6 6 5 3 3
```

Call:

windscreen wiper	A
open left window	B
put on handbrake	C
pull the button that says 'Push Heater'	D
open right window	E
high-pitched scream	p
rumble	q
dull thud	r

Then we have:

B, C, E	→	p, q	(i)
A, C, D, E	→	q, r	(ii)
A, B, C, D	→	p, r	(iii)
A, B, C, E	→	p, q, r	(iv)

(Remember that if, for example, B → p then whenever p is on the right B must be on the left, and when p is *not* on the right B *cannot* be on the left.)

Let us look for where p is not.

In (ii) p is not on the right, ∴ p is not caused by A, C, D or E. ∴ p must be caused by B (and we check by seeing that B is on the left in (i), (iii) and (iv)).

In (iii) q is not on the right, ∴ q is not caused by A, B, C or D. ∴ q must be caused by E (and we check by seeing that E is on the left in (i), (ii) and (iv)).

From (iv) D cannot be the cause of p, q or r.

And in (i) r is not on the right, ∴ r is not caused by B, C or E.

∴ r must be caused by A (and we check by seeing that A is on the left in (ii), (iii) and (iv)).

Complete solution

 The high-pitched scream is caused by opening the left window.

 The rumble is caused by opening the right window.

 The dull thud is caused by the windscreen wiper.

146   The Richer the Truer

Suppose that B(2) is true. Then A(2) must be true. (They both say the same thing.) ∴ C must be a Wotta-Woppa, and C's wages are 4 Hopes more than A's. But this is not possible for C is a Wotta-Woppa. ∴ our assumption is false, and B(2) and A(2) are both false. ∴ C must be a Pukka (no one else can be).
∴ C(1) true, ∴ B's wages are less than A's, ∴ A is a Shilli-Shalla and B is a Wotta-Woppa.
∴ A(1) is true and B(1) false.

 From A(1), C's wages are a multiple of 3, and from C(2) (true) C's wages are even.

∴ C's wages are 36, 30 or less. But they cannot be 30 or less, for B's wages would then be 20 Hopes or less, which is too small.

∴ C's wages are 36, B's are 24 and from C(1) A's wages are 27.

Complete solution

 A is a Shilli-Shalla; his wages are 27 Hopes.

 B is a Wotta-Woppa; his wages are 24 Hopes.

 C is a Pukka; his wages are 36 Hopes.

147 Uncle Bungle Multiplies

$$
\begin{array}{ccccc}
(a) & (b) & (c) & (d) & (e) \\
 & 1 & 6 & 6 & 3 \\
 & & & & 3 \\
\hline
2 & 1 & 3 & 7 & 9 \\
\hline
\end{array}
$$

The last figure in the answer can only be 8. To get 8 the first figure in (e) could be 4, and the second could be 2; or the first figure in (e) could be 2 and the second could be 4. But if the second figure in (e) were 2, then, since the first figure in (b) can only be 2, there would be only four figures, not five, in the answer. ∴ in (e), the second 3 must be 4, and the first must be 2.

If the first figure in (d) was 5, then the second would have to be 0; but it cannot be. ∴ the first figure in (d) is 7, and the second is 8. (Note that there is now 2 to carry.)

If the first figure in (c) was 7, then the second would have to be 8+2, but it is 2 or 4. But if the first figure in (c) was 5, then the second would be 0+2, which is all right.

The first figure in (b) must be 2; ∴ the first two figures of the answer must be 8+2 = 10.

Complete solution

$$
\begin{array}{ccccc}
 & 2 & 5 & 7 & 2 \\
 & & & & 4 \\
\hline
1 & 0 & 2 & 8 & 8 \\
\hline
\end{array}
$$

148 Football

Four Teams, New Method

The points which A, B, C and D got might be divided as follows:

	Wins or draws	Goals
A	5	2
B	10	3
C	15	5
D	—	4

Each team played at least one game for they all got some points. If the wins and draws were as above, then three games were played ($5+10+15 = 30$). And there cannot be more. If only two games were played then no team could have played more than one, and C would have got at least 10 points for goals.

∴ three games were played, and the table above is correct.

We are told that at least 2 goals were scored by each side in a drawn match. ∴ B cannot have got their points from two draws (they would then have got at least 14 points).

∴ A v. C was a draw, and B and C both won one (three matches altogether). And with 4 goals and no points D must have been beaten by both B and C. ∴ A only played once (against C), and the score was 2–2.

C v. D was 3–?. And B v. D was 3–?. And since D lost both these matches and scored 4 goals, ∴ the score in each was 3–2.

Complete solution

    A v. C   2–2
    B v. D   3–2
    C v. D   3–2

149 Addition

Letters for Digits, Three Numbers

	(a)	(b)	(c)	(d)	(e)
	L	P	B	R	R
	T	L	S	R	R
	S	B	R	R	R
	R	L	M	P	L

Consider (a). R must be at least 6 (1+2+3). But if R were 6, then in (e) L would be 8; but L in (a) cannot be 8. ∴ R is not 6.

If R were 9, then in (e) L would be 7; but L in (a) cannot be 7. ∴ R is not 9. ∴ R is 7 or 8.

Suppose R = 7. Then L in (e) would be 1 (3×7 = 21); and P in (d) would be 3 ((3×7)+2 = 23). In (b) we would have: 3(P)+1(L)+B+(0, 1 or 2 to carry) = 10+1(L), (so that there would be 1 to carry to (a); but not 2, for B would then have to be more than 10). ∴ T and S would be between them 2 and 3. But we are assuming that P = 3. ∴ our assumption is wrong. ∴ R must be 8. ∴ L = 4. ∴ P = 6. And, since L = 4 and there is one to carry to (a), T and S must be between them 1 and 2.

In (b), since 2 is T or S and 4 is L, B must be 3. And in (c), since M cannot be 4, M must be 5, and S = 2, T = 1.

Complete solution

```
  4 6 3 8 8
  1 4 2 8 8
  2 3 8 8 8
 ──────────
  8 4 5 6 4
```

Suppose B's statement is true. Then D must be a Pukka (B having made a true statement is at least a Shilli-Shalla). ∴ A is a Pukka (see D's statement). But this is not possible for it makes two Pukkas. ∴ our assumption is incorrect, ∴ B's statement is false and B must be a Shilli-Shalla (he has made a false statement and either belongs to a more truthful tribe than D in which case he is a Shilli-Shalla, or belongs to a tribe that is as truthful as D in which case also he must be a Shilli-Shalla for this is the only tribe which has two representatives).

Suppose D's statement is true. Then D must be a Shilli-Shalla, and A is a Pukka, ∴ A's statement is true and C is a Shilli-Shalla. But this makes three Shilli-Shallas, ∴ D's statement is false, ∴ A is not a Pukka, ∴ C is a Pukka (no one else can be). ∴ D is not a Shilli-Shalla, ∴ D must be a Wotta-Woppa, and A must be the other Shilli-Shalla.

Complete solution
  A is a Shilli-Shalla;
  B is a Shilli-Shalla;
  C is a Pukka;
  D is a Wotta-Woppa.

More non-fiction in Puffins

CARS, BOATS, TRAINS AND PLANES
CASTLES, CHURCHES AND HOUSES
Alan Jamieson

Two books designed to help children recognize objects and buildings they see when travelling about the countryside and towns, on holiday or in a car. (*Originals*)

PUMA PUZZLES
Michael Holt and Peter Edwards

A collection of simple mazes, visual and mathematical puzzles. (*Original*)

THE PUFFIN SOCCER QUIZ BOOK
David Prole

Many questions to test your knowledge of the game. (*Original*)

THE YOUNG PUFFIN BOOK OF PICTURE PUZZLES
Rowan Barnes-Murphy

A hundred funny and often mystifying picture puzzles, to make younger children laugh and also think. (*Original*)

A colourful col...ROUND
year. Month by month th... do throughout the
and do, appropriate to the mont... for things to make

THE PUFFIN BOOK OF CAR GAMES
Douglas P. St P. Bernard

A bumper collection of over 100 games to play and things to
do while you are travelling. (*Original*)

RECYCLOPEDIA*
Robin Symons

There's always something useful to be made out of old
rubbish – here are many different suggestions.

COOKING IS A GAME YOU CAN EAT*
Fay Maschler

Delicious recipes for all kinds of food, to be cooked indoors
and out.

*Not available in the U.S.A.

CODES FOR

Burton Albert Jr.

A fascinating collecti...
7 to 11. Snoop-d...round your...
secret m...